FAITH, HOPE & PERSEVERANCE

An Adoptee's Journey
To Finding Her Biological Family

DIANE GRAY

outskirts
press

Outskirts Press, Inc.
http://www.outskirtspress.com

ISBN: 978-1-9772-2664-8

Library of Congress Control Number: 2020908202

PRINTED IN THE UNITED STATES OF AMERICA

This book is dedicated to my children, grandchildren, great grandchildren and generations yet to come. It is a story of my family, my journey to find my biological family, my roots, but more importantly a story of love.

My journey to find my biological family has been an emotional roller coaster that spans over 50 years. More importantly, it is a story of how Faith, Hope and Perseverance kept me going.

I love you all to the moon and back.

"The more YOU know of YOUR HISTORY the more liberated you are."

Maya Angelou

TABLE OF CONTENTS

Introduction

Mark Twain said, "The two most important days in your life are the day you are born and the day you find out why". Adoptees have the right to know who they are. It is our human right. As infants we lost the choice but if we decide to search we take back that choice.

I call myself northern by birth, southern by choice. My adoptive parents held me in their arms on the fifth day of my life in upstate New York in 1955. I was their second child to be adopted. My sister Ann was a few months old when she was adopted. Ann is five years older than me. Can you imagine what a thrill it would be for a husband and wife who couldn't naturally have children of their own to be able to hold a child in their arms they could call their own? At the age of five I was told I was adopted and never really thought about it much until I was in high school. I remember sitting at the kitchen table with my mom and my best friend Cheryl. Cheryl and I asked my mom if she knew anything about my birth parents. The only thing my mom said was that she was a secretary. It was noticeably clear that my mother was becoming uncomfortable with the whole subject. When asked why my parents couldn't have children, my mother got really upset. All she would say was that she couldn't say because it would embarrass my father. Then she stormed out of the room.

It wasn't until I had my own children in 1974 and 1981 that I really wanted to know about any of my family medical history. I remember being somewhat embarrassed that I was unable to give my side of the family's medical history. The only medical history I could give the doctors was their father's side. All I could whisper was that I was adopted. I always thought there was negative connotations to being adopted. Somewhere there was someone that didn't want me. I was given up. I wasn't good enough.

Yes, I was given up. I was given up for a better life, probably something my birth mother couldn't have given me. Yes, I am a blessed child of God to be put in the arms of my adoptive parents.

When talking to others about adoption who are not adopted, they have a hard time relating to how we feel. They don't understand why we have a hard time not looking like anyone else in our family. They don't understand why we are always trying to please our family, our spouse, our children, our employers and our friends. Why? Because of fear of rejection and abandonment. It seems only other adoptees really "get it".

Over the past ten years science and technology have made it much easier to help adoptees find their biological family. I'm sure you've seen TV shows like Long Lost Family. If it wasn't for the internet and DNA testing companies, it would probably be much harder to find family. Millions and millions of adoptees and others looking for lost family members have spit in a tube or swabbed the inside of their cheek to get answers. DNA testing is the number one source for adoptees looking for biological family. It is estimated that over twenty six million consumers have taken a DNA test as of early 2019.

One might say that the decision to look for biological family takes nerves of steel and it's not for the faint of heart. I would have to agree. There's so many variables. You really need to be ready to accept just about anything that comes up. I always dreamed my biological family would welcome me with open arms. Some adoptees go through so much rejection. Families may reject adoptees because of a deep dark family secret and that adoptee may have unlocked that secret. Some birth mothers just want to forget the child they gave away because they've moved on with their lives and don't want their current spouse finding out their secret from the past. Whatever the circumstances are, you just need to be prepared for one heck of a roller coaster ride. You never know what will fall out of your family tree.

Ever since I was told I was special and adopted, I always thought about "the other family". Why was I given up for adoption? Did I do something wrong? Was I supposed to be a boy and not a girl? I loved my parents and I always wanted to please them. I would entertain them with little plays I had written and sing songs I heard on the radio. My parents loved it and said I was a great actress. Even though I was a happy girl, the images of another family kept coming to the front of my mind.

It was mid-year of 1969 when my father's job took us from upstate New York to Virginia. I was devastated. How could my parents make me leave the only home I knew? I was being uprooted from aunts, uncles, cousins and friends I had ever since elementary school. And to make matters worse, I would be starting high school at a new school.

In 1969, the world was really changing. We were watching the chilling events of the Vietnam war unfold before our eyes on television. We saw death and destruction on the evening news all while eating dinner. The images are still with me to this day. We witnessed mankind take the first steps on the moon. We watched war protests, civil rights protests, and the biggest rock concert of our time, Woodstock.

I started my freshman year of high school in September, 1969. To me, it was horrible. Our school was a fairly new building. As I walked the halls, I hung my head down. I didn't want to make friends. I wanted to go home to New York and graduate with the friends I had grown up with. I wouldn't talk to anyone. I remember going to the girl's bathroom between classes and getting cornered by several black girls. I happened to be wearing a red dress that day. They said it was ugly and they were going to beat me up. They said I was a damn Yankee, wasn't wanted here and that I should go home. I was scared out of my mind. Someone walked in and told the girls to leave me alone. My heart was racing and I was terrified. I wish I knew who that person was so I could thank them. The girls left the bathroom and I went to my next class. I will never forget that day. This was my first time ever being bullied. I went home and told my mother what happened. I was crying so hard I could hardly tell her what had happened. Mom called the school and told them what happened. I don't remember what was said but I do know that no one else bothered me after that. I always tried my best to be the good daughter, tried to please my parents afraid I might be "relinquished" back. My parents always loved me. They told me often. This is just one of the fears adoptees feel. It's somehow wired in our DNA.

It took me over six months before I started socializing and began to make friends. I remember thinking that "my other family" would have never uprooted me like this. "My other family" would have never put me through all this. I could easily see my other family in my mind but there were no faces. There was always a lot of them. At that time, I never knew why God would plant these images in my mind. I know God would reveal what was true in His time. I knew my parents loved me and wanted to protect me but the images of "my other family" would become stronger the older I got.

Each birthday I wondered if "my other family" would think of me. I would always close my eyes and make the same wish every year as I blew out the candles on my birthday cake. As the smoke from the candles disappeared, I wondered if this would be the year I would finally meet my family? These images haunted me often. At Christmas time I would think about "my other family" and visualize a tree beautifully decorated with lots of presents under it. I could almost smell fresh baked cookies coming out of the oven and hear packages being ripped opened and squeals of excitement. But these feelings seemed to fade just as quickly as they came.

My most vivid images would always be of a family seated around a kitchen table. A mother was seated at one end and a father at the other.

The images of these memories were of three girls and one boy. There was always a lot of food on the table and always laughter, lots of laughter. My images would come quickly and disappear just as quickly. One thing was for sure, they always made me happy.

Sometimes while outside watching the stars on a clear night, I would wonder if "my other family" was looking at the same stars I was. When I was at the beach, I wondered if "my other family" loved the beach as much as I do. Most importantly, I wondered if I looked anything like "my other family".

When I was younger, I often asked myself how a woman could ever give up her child. Was she a teenager and just didn't know how to take care of an infant? Or maybe she just couldn't deal with a child for whatever reason. That child is their flesh and blood. This sounds rather harsh but I was just an elementary kid. Growing older, I realized these ideas were ridiculous. Some girls I went to high school were pregnant when they walked the stage for graduation. I didn't give it another thought.

As I aged….ok….let's say "matured" I realized adoption wasn't really a bad thing at all. I was smart, clothes on my back, a roof over my head and was loved unconditionally by my parents. In the past several years as I opened up conversations concerning my search, I heard some amazing stories about other adoptees who were also searching for biological family and women who "relinquished" their child for various reasons.

Let's face it. A child will change everything in a person's life. Adoption for a young woman is a great option so she can continue on her life plan. A single mother would have to put the child's needs first which would limit herself to develop professionally. It takes a lot of energy to care for an infant and raise a child. And let's not forget about how much it costs to raise a child. According to the U.S. Department of Agriculture, February 26, 2018, it takes about $233,000 to raise a child to the age of 18. This doesn't even include college. By relinquishing her child through the proper channels, this young woman would be giving her child the greatest gift of love.

Adoption is not expensive. Often, the birth mother's pregnancy costs and some living expenses will be covered in most states by sponsorship of the adoptive family. Some agencies charge a minimal $20 for a background check for the foster to adoption process.

An open adoption is another option. This allows the biological mother the opportunity to be a part of the child's life. Open adoption is very popular. The adoptive family and birth mother work out a plan to keep in contact.

I was born and adopted in New York State which is a closed adoption state. All records are sealed. My birth certificate has my adoptive parents listed. It wasn't until I applied for my non-identifying information from New York that I learned a few pieces of information surrounding my birth. I will go into more detailed about non-identification information in a later chapter.

A study sponsored by the U.S. Department of Education shows that adopted children have positive effects.

- Children were reported with excellent physical health as the rest of the population.
- The same amount described themselves as close and happy with their parents.
- Adopted children are more likely to be read and told stories to than other children.
- Adopted children are more likely to participate in after-school activities.

Of course, all these wonderful qualities depend on the kind of environment the child is raised in.

There are many adoptive families who can't physically have children and want to give a child a loving home. There are screening processes and the birth mother can often choose an adoptive family. Adoption is a beautiful option. Birth mothers have options.

After I found my biological family, I felt God tap me on the shoulder and made it very clear to me to write a book about my experience. This is my story of how faith, hope and perseverance helped me find my biological family.

Chapter 1

Chapter 1

THE GLUE

I STOOD AT the podium in a chapel at a funeral home in Central Virginia in 2009. I had just heard a beautiful message delivered to the congregation by my two sons Ben and Adam. The sweet music of "Carry the Cross" had just been sung by my husband William. It was amazing to see how many family and friends had come to remember my mother in spite of the snow accumulating outside. The chapel was quiet and it was my turn to deliver the eulogy on behalf of my sister and myself. I've never had to do this before. I didn't write any notes. I just wanted to speak from the heart. I stood up straight, scanned the room, found my composure and looked straight at my sister. "We're the lucky ones. We were chosen." I explained how fortunate we were to be adopted by our parents. I told a few funny stories about my mother and her baking skills. She always made scrumptious cookies by the hundreds during holidays. I could almost smell fresh baked cookies coming out of the oven as I stood there.

After the memorial service the family gathered at my mother's apartment. Ann and I started talking about our adoptions. Did mom leave any clues? Was there some paperwork stashed away in storage that we could find? The search was on. I went upstairs to mom's storage and ransacked everything there. I found old photos, my old report cards from elementary school, some of my father's belongings from his career and lots and lots of Christmas ornaments and decorations but no adoption papers. Ann searched the apartment and found nothing! We decided to deal with moms belongs. Going through mom's crazy collections of porcelain dolls that she had made, china, jewelry, photos and cookbooks was quite an ordeal. Still no paperwork about our adoptions were found. We spent the next few days packing, loading furniture and cleaning. During this tedious process we'd tell stories of good times and bad. We'd laugh and we'd cry. It was time for all of us to head home. Ann and her family to upstate New York, me and my family to Eastern North Carolina and Virginia. It was sad that the glue that had held us all together was gone. How my mother actually died is still a mystery to this day. Ann and I were not even aware mom had been in the hospital and that whatever her illness was would lead to her unexpected death.

My parents had decided years ago that the upkeep of their beautiful home was just too much. My father's health started to decline. There were just too many chores that my mother had to manage while taking care of my father's needs. They made the decision to move to a retirement community that would accommodate all levels of health needs. It was clean, well-staffed, meal menus seemed good and healthy and everyone, including the residents were amazing. My parents even knew several of them. It was at this retirement community my mother learned to use a computer. We were all so proud of her. She had made a binder of all the email jokes she ever received. Mom even taught several others how to email their families. There was always socializing going on, card games and bingo in the game room and residents could learn new craft skills. On many occasions they would have local musicians come and perform for them. And of course, there was always a church service and lots of prayers. This retirement home seemed to be a great place for them and they were happy.

My father's health had been steadily deteriorating. My mother would call me crying many times. Dad couldn't recognize mom some days. He couldn't tell you what he had for breakfast. He would often tell you the same story over and over, some stories were from his early childhood. He would tell us the story of rolling a whiskey barrel down the street with his fraternity brothers and how they really got in big trouble by the police. His mind was slipping away and this became very difficult for my mom. I would come see her and dad as much as possible. My friends and ex-husband whom my parents deeply love, would come over and help.

Christmas was right around the corner. My father's health continued to decline. My sister and I thought it would be best to spend the holiday with our parents. We knew the stress and sadness would be hanging in the air so we thought we'd bring as much joy and laughter as we could. My mom was really glad to see us. She looked so tired. It looked like she had aged 10 years. We felt helpless. My father seemed to have a recollection of who we all were. He even asked us why we were there. We told him it was Christmas and that we wanted to spend it with him and mom. I will never forget that sweet smile he gave us that day. His eyes just lit up. That was the best Christmas gift ever. Tears were streaming down our cheeks as we took our fathers hands. The next minute he didn't even know who we were. This was heart wrenching. How had my mother been able to cope day in and day out like this? My father was physically shrinking away to nothing. He couldn't remember how to eat and we had to coach him how to drink through a straw.

After my father had fallen asleep that night, our mom talked about how much of a struggle things had been. We didn't realize it and we didn't know. She also warned us that it wouldn't be long before he died. She was happy we were there for her but she hated that we had to see our father in this condition. Our father had always been strong. He was well educated, devoted to his family and an avid sportsman. To see him like this, a shrunken man in a fetal position was difficult for us to watch.

Later that night my sister and I decided to try and put a little holiday spirit in the house. We put together a plan and the next morning we'd start decorating, make cookies and put on some Christmas music. Right after breakfast we told mom we would make cookies and get out the Christmas decorations. She said "no" and she wanted no part of Christmas this year. I looked at my sister with a raised eyebrow and a smile and told her "yes we were". We told dad we were going to the grocery store and asked what he would like. He said shrimp and pudding. Much to my mother's chagrin, we took an inventory of what we'd need from the grocery store. Mom said no shrimp. She said dad can't eat it. Off we go…we get to spend a little sister time together. Even if it wasn't the best circumstances, we decided to make this a fun trip. We not only got all the ingredients to make moms favorite cookies, we also got Santa hats and stockings and shrimp for dad. This was going to be fun.

We get back to mom and dad's apartment and dad was sitting at the kitchen table. He couldn't believe all the food we brought back. We didn't let him see the shrimp. I quietly put it in the refrigerator for him to hopefully enjoy later on Christmas day.

It was Christmas Eve. Let the baking begin! My sister who is a phenomenal cook was in charge. She made so many kinds of cookies. I loved the rum balls, thumb print and chocolate chip cookies the best. I can still smell the heaven sent cookies baking in the oven. As my sister was cooking away in the kitchen, I went up to mom and dad's storage to get the Christmas decorations. Since their apartment was small, they really didn't have much. I took everything I could find. There was a table top tree, ornaments and lights. I even found a wreath for their front door. JACKPOT! I remember having to make a few trips but I sure didn't mind. We couldn't wait for mom and dad to see what we had planned.

While mom and dad were napping, we decorated their home. We had so much fun. Between the wonderful smell of the fresh baked cookies and the decorations, we transformed their apartment into a Christmas showcase with what we had. After decorating, my sister and I had a chance to talk. It was hard to be away from our own families during the holidays and we talked about how much we missed them. We both agreed we were exactly where we were supposed to be, right here, in mom and dad's apartment on Christmas. Our conversation turned to Christmas' past. We laughed about having to trudge through knee deep snow to find the right tree when we lived in upstate New York. We laughed about how cold it was all the while arguing about which tree was perfect.

Being the youngest, I really didn't care which tree it was. I was cold and I wanted to go home and decorate whatever tree was chopped down. I remember my dad chopping down the tree, dragging it through the snow and tying it down to the top of the car. Once we got the tree home, my father would put it in the tree stand. To me I thought it took forever. He had to cut a little off the bottom, place the tree in the stand, make sure the angel would fit on the top, meticulously straighten the tree then add water. It took what seemed like hours. I wonder if anyone ever counted the eye rolls my sister and I would do.

Mom woke up from her nap. Despite the fact she didn't want any decorations I know she was pleased. We even saw a twinkle in her eye. She knew we worked hard. I can't remember what we had for dinner that day but I can tell you what my dad had....SHRIMP! He sat down at the table and we all put on our Santa hats. He was very aware of what was going on. I know God was blessing all of us. We gave him the shrimp thinking he would only have a few. Nope! He ate the whole pound and loved every bite. He said it was the best he had ever had. There were plenty of smiles and tears going around during that dinner. Even though I can't tell you what we ate other than dad's shrimp and pudding, it was the best dinner I have ever had. To see my father being "in the present" for just a little while was the best Christmas present ever.

A few days later it was time for my sister and me to head back home to our families and me to my job. It was the hardest thing to do. Barring any unforeseen circumstances, it would take my sister about ten hours to get home and about four hours for me. We were all pretty exhausted but that didn't matter. We made memories. Memories that will be with us forever.

It was the first week of February, 2007 when I got the call from my mother. She said dad had been taken to the hospital and not expected to live much longer. Dad had developed kidney issues. This is part of the heartbreak of dementia as your brain forgets to tell other parts of the body what it needs to do. I will never forget the last day I saw my father. Instead of going to my mother's home, I decided to drive straight to the hospital. All I could hear was my mother telling me he didn't have long to live. I rushed up to his room, opened the door and there he was, sitting up and eating dinner. He was in great spirits and had a smile on his face that I had seen in pictures of him when he was a little boy. My first thoughts was that he didn't look like he was about to leave this earth. He looked great. He had color in his cheeks, a smile on his face and he was eating. He even asked what I was doing here and said he was fine. I gave him a kiss on the cheek and said that I came to see him. He asked how Ben and Adam were, we talked about the weather, and we had a few laughs about the food in the hospital. Most importantly, it was just the two of us. He asked me how mom was. I assured him she was fine. I knew mom was a wreck but I didn't want dad to worry. I wanted him to focus on his health. I knew my dad's situation was very serious but at that moment, he was having a moment of pure clarity. He knew where he was, he knew I was there, he knew he could have a conversation with me, and I knew he loved me.

Dad knew it was getting dark outside. He had a thing about "his girls" driving at night. Dad was always very protective of "his girls".

To appease dad I said OK. We were holding hands during our visit together. His grip was weak yet strong at the same time. I gave dad a kiss on the cheek, said goodbye, told him that I loved him and walked toward the door.

As I was walking towards the door, something told me to turn around. I turned around and looked at my dad. I saw a man of strength, I saw a man in peace, I saw a man of integrity, and I saw a man who loved God. He said to me "one more thing". I said "sure dad anything". He said "will you take care of your mother?" I remember saying "you know I will". I gave him a big smile and walked out the door. That was the last time I saw my dad.

I headed to my mother's home. I kept replaying dad's visit over and over in my mind. It made me smile, it made me laugh and it made me cry. My father's death was very near.

I pulled into the parking lot and knew I needed to pull myself together. I didn't want mom to see how upset I was and that I had been crying. I walked to the home, passed the receptionists desk and hit the number "2" on the elevator. I thanked God that no one else was on the elevator because those precious moments on the elevator were very quiet and peaceful. I walked down the hall to my mom's apartment. I couldn't help but notice how beautifully decorated the area around my mom's door was. She had an unusual collection of gift bags she had saved over the years. This particular display of gift bags seemed to have all the colors of the rainbow and matching bows. All the residents decorated around their doors with wreaths, plants, pictures or anything else they thought was beautiful. Mom always seemed to have a knack for decorating but this door display was one of her best. It made me smile. I knocked on the door. Mom and my sister were there.

I knew in my heart that our visit would probably not turn out to be the happiest but I made a promise to myself that I would make it as fun as I possibly could despite the circumstances. I think my sister was feeling the same way too. I told her that I had just left the hospital and what a great talk dad and I had. I also told her dad had a little color in his cheeks. She explained that he had been in the care of hospice which was a relief to her as she got the help she needed for him. Mom explained how great they had been. She looked tired and worn out. We all decided to get dinner and go to bed early so we could get to the hospital and hopefully catch up with dad's doctor during rounds.

The next morning we all had coffee, breakfast and we were getting ready to go to the hospital. The phone rang, my mother answered it and started to cry. My sister and I look at each other. We knew what had happened. Dad was gone.

We stood in the kitchen hugging each other, consoling each other and crying. I thanked God for giving me the opportunity to have my time with dad the day before. Now I had a promise to fulfill to my dad…to take care of mom.

My mind was racing. We need to talk about funeral arrangements. We need to find the will. Will mom want to stay in this apartment? The list in my head went on and on. But first I need to get mom to the hospital.

The drive to the hospital still remains a blur to me. I do remember walking into my dad's room. No one was allowed to enter except my mom, my sister and myself. What I saw was a beautiful send off for my dad's journey to Heaven. My dad was lying on the bed looking so very peaceful. It was the kind of peace I had never seen before. Everything in the room was beautiful and pristine. On the television there was beautiful music playing and amazing pictures of scenes across America. There were flowers too. It was though he engineered all this for the benefit of mom and "his girls". Maybe it was a sign of how beautiful the start of ones journey to Heaven can really be. Maybe it was dad's way of telling us everything is going to be fine and God's in control.

We each said our goodbyes to dad. My mother, sister and I sat in the room for quite some time. We laughed, we cried, we reminisced. All the while I kept thinking about the last words my dad spoke to me, "take care of your mother". What will I do? I live four hours away. How can I manage being so far away? What about doctor's appointments, getting prescriptions filled, getting groceries? What if she falls? Mom had been dad's caregiver for as long as she was physically able and was a registered nurse. I wasn't sure if being a caregiver to my mom was in my DNA. But this isn't about me. It was about taking care of my mom while fulfilling dad's wishes for his funeral.

When we left the hospital room, the very sweet nurse who had been taking care of dad stopped us and said she was in the room when dad died and how peaceful it was. We thanked her for her kindness and care of our father. I really wish I could recall her name because she was a true angel.

I truly don't remember much of my dad's funeral except he was cremated. Mom had decided she didn't want dad's remains and told Ann and I that we could have them. I remember the day my sister and I went to get the remains. We drove to the funeral home exchanging our thoughts about moms care but didn't come up with anything conclusive. We walked into the funeral home, told them who we were and why we were there. The woman said she would be right back with the remains. My sister and I were walking around and stumbled into what looked like a gift shop. Humor never ceases to amaze me. Humor has a way of creeping up on you in some crazy places. This particular gift shop in this particular funeral home just happened to creep up on both my sister and I at the same moment. There were all kinds of flags, blankets, jewelry and clothing….okay…I get that. Some families have lots of different traditions. But personalized stationary, post cards? I get it now but it seemed really crazy to my sister and I at that time. I think God needed us to have a good laugh. God has to have a sense of humor for us to have a good laugh in a gift shop at a funeral home.

Here comes our greeter with a nice box with dad's remains. It was carefully wrapped. But we need it divided so my sister could have half and I would have the other half. My sister speaks up and says "can we get this divided in half? My sister wants half and I want the other half". The look on the woman's face was priceless. She said they had never had a request like that. I thought to myself "today's the day sunshine".

About fifteen minutes later she came back. The remains had been re-packaged into two nice boxes. My sister got her nice box in a plastic bag from the hospital and I got my nice box in a plastic grocery bag. I can only imagine what happened when the lady went back to complete our request. I'm hoping they have some kind of sense of humor.

We took our plastic bags with dad's remains and got back in the car. We both needed a good laugh and this certainly was a doozie. We never told mom. Little did I know that sometime later these remains would be a very important moment in my life!

Chapter 2

—❧—

LIFE AFTER DAD

IN KEEPING WITH my promise to my dad to "take care of my mother" both my sister and I would call her every day. Mom looked forward to our calls and would tell us what was going on in her retirement community. She told us what she had for lunch and dinner, the latest gossip and asked what was going on in our lives. I would travel to see her every other weekend. On one particular weekend my mom proudly showed me "her office." Her office was in a small room off the craft and hobby room. It was slightly larger than a broom closet. In this office was a desk with a computer, a printer, chair and a bookshelf. The room was surprisingly well lit. Mom sat down at her desk and I grabbed a chair from the craft room. Next thing I knew, mom fired up the computer and carefully entered her password, humming all the while. She pulled up her email and showed it to me. She was looking for "the joke of the day." Mom printed out every joke she received in her email and cataloged them in a huge binder. She even showed me how to forward it.

I told mom how proud I was of her for learning something new, especially something in previous years she thought was too hard. She said she was self-taught. I think she had a little help from some of the ladies at the front desk. The girls at the front desk truly loved mom. Mom would help other residents email their families. She always had a big heart and always helped others.

God really has a sense of humor. Mom would ask me about my love life. I would tell her I wasn't looking for a relationship now. I just wasn't ready. My mother told me I would never meet the right man in a bar.

Several months later I was at work and having one of those days where things just didn't go right at all. Christmas was right around the corner and I had not done any shopping. My friend Tracy called me and right away she knew I was feeling a little blue. She said she'd be over in a few minutes and for me to get ready to go out. I told her I didn't feel like it but she persisted. Reluctantly, I went and we went to a bar for a few drinks. My friend Tracy has always been such a good friend and she knew I needed to get out and have fun. It was about a week and a half before Christmas, 2006 and we were going to spread some holiday cheer. We get to the bar and there was a man on the stage playing music. WOW…he was awesome. I asked Tracy who he was and she said she didn't know. My reply was "seriously, you know everyone!" I want to find out who he is. I love his music. I went to the dance floor and just stood there listening to his awesome music. Thinking back on that day I must have looked like a complete geek. You know the type, eyes fixed on him, mouth open. I must have looked like a lunatic. Apparently, I'm not a lunatic because he took a break and walked right over to me. I'm thinking….oh boy…here we go. He's really handsome, tall and dressed in black, what am I going to say? And I'm not ever short on words! He said hi first. I told him I really liked his music. I felt like a total geek. But somehow as we continued talking about where we worked and what we did, talking to William seemed to get easier. Then we talked about where each of us lived. We lived in the same apartment community. BINGO! He was a breath of fresh air. I knew there was something very special about William. His break was up and he needed to get back on stage. By the end of the night we had exchanged phone numbers. I didn't think he would call but I gave him my number anyway. After all, since it was so close to Christmas, people get busy. Low and behold, a few days later, William called.

We started our new relationship slowly. On Saturday mornings William would come over for coffee and breakfast. He would bring flowers. We both loved drinking coffee and getting to know each better. Our relationship was growing.

I had told William about my dad's death, that I was adopted, from upstate New York originally, grew up in Virginia, my two sons and about my mom. I even told him about my dad's ashes. William was very easy to talk to, very supportive and compassionate. I knew he was special. William told me about growing up in a small town in Eastern North Carolina, about his son and daughter, his job and his parents. I knew we had many things in common even though we came from different parts of the country. Our basic upbringing was somewhat similar. We both were brought up by Christian parents. God knew what he was doing by bringing the two of us together.

Our relationship continued to grow. Two things I knew had to be done. The first was for William to meet my mother. The second was to place my dad's ashes in the Blue Ridge Mountains in Virginia. After my dad retired, he was a volunteer ranger at the Blue Ridge Mountains. He loved it and that's where he wanted his ashes placed.

I explained to William about my dad's wish to have his ashes placed in the Blue Ridge Mountains. I told him that dad had been a volunteer park ranger there for many years working in many capacities. With tears in my eyes I told William I was ready to let dad go and place his ashes in the mountains. He agreed and wanted to know when. I told him it wasn't far from where my mother lived and asked he would like to meet her. To me, when you're in a new relationship, it's best if you just speak from the heart and see where things go. Meeting parents can be somewhat unnerving. But not this time. I called mom and made arrangements. I told her I was bringing William. I did not tell her about the ashes as she did not want to ever know when we carried out dad's wish. She was excited to see me and meet William. My problem was trying to figure out how to tell mom we would be out during the afternoon. I told her I was going to show William around town.

The weather in early spring in the mountains can be a roll of the dice. William and I were willing to take the risk. I packed up dad's ashes and placed them in a back pack before we left for the weekend. It seemed a cold front was coming through as we drove to the Blue Ridge Mountains. The weather had gotten colder and it was raining a little. We got out of the car, I bring the backpack with my dad's ashes and we start the hike up the mountain. They used to have a bus that would take you to the top and you can hike back down but the bus wasn't available until May. It was March. This was going to be a cold, wet hike up the mountain. I questioned whether or not we should go but we decided we should. After all, we'd already driven four hours to my mothers. What's a little hike up a mountain, right? HA! I knew I was out of shape but when you combine the cold, rain and rugged terrain it just seemed to magnify how out of shape I really was.

We both agreed it was a miserable hike but William kept encouraging me to go. We had gone about two thirds of the way to the top when we stopped. I looked up and saw the most beautiful view of the Blue Ridge Mountains. I told William this is it. It's the perfect spot. The rain had let up and the sun seemed to be shining on the mountain. The earthy smell from the rain really gave me the assurance that this was the right place. Dad would have loved it. Even the leaves were shiny from the rain drops. Despite the fact that I was cold, wet and terribly out of shape, I knew this was the perfect spot! So I pulled the ashes out of my back pack, opened the box to find yet another box. I told William I had never seen human ashes before and that I had never spread any ones ashes out before. He had never done it either. Ah! A first for us and we're doing it together. Since this was our first time we talked about how to do this. First the wind direction had to be right. We sure didn't want a change of direction of the wind and have the ashes blown back on us. Do we say a prayer? The wind seemed to be blowing in the right direction. The wet, earthy fragrance of fresh rain reminded me how my father always loved that smell. Rain drops were falling ever so slowly off the leaves. I said a few words and a prayer and the ashes magically went through the air. I watched and was amazed at the beauty of the whole experience. It was at the exact moment of the release of the ashes that I fell in love with William. This is the importance of the ashes and a life changing experience I referred to earlier.

I could have never carried out my father's wishes without William by my side. He motivated and encouraged me along the way. That day changed my life forever as he is the man I married in July, 2008. It is a day in my life that I will never forget. What makes me sad is that I could not tell mom. She did not want to know what Ann and I did with the ashes. Ann and I never knew why mom didn't want to know about the whereabouts of dad's ashes. She would never say. We thought mom may have wanted to remember dad when he was healthy and whole.

Mom was adapting to being alone but really missed dad. During one of our conversations she had mentioned her new friend Cathy. Cathy had stopped in to visit about once a week, she was a newly ordained minister and a Certified Financial Planner. Cathy had even invited my mother to her ordination. My mother did go and told us about how beautiful the ceremony was. Mom really enjoyed Cathy's visits. Cathy had "volunteered" to help mom with a new will, paperwork to prove to the retirement community management that she could still afford to live in the community since my father had died. She even helped with life insurance policies my dad had and helped mom balance her checkbook. My sister and I never thought anything about it. Fasten your seat belts…things are going to get a little crazy here.

Cathy had told mom that her daughters couldn't be executrix of mom's estate because we both lived out of state. In my mind red flags were going up about Cathy and what was she really up to? Now I don't know a lot about wills and legal things but I do know anyone can be appointed to execute a will. It doesn't matter what state you live in. My mother believed everything Cathy said. She thought that since Cathy was ordained and a Certified Financial Planner that she knew how it all worked. Both my sister and I tried to tell mom that that's not right. To no avail, she didn't listen to us.

My sister and I decided that we would both spend more time with mom. Ann drove down from upstate New York and I drove up from North Carolina. We had her call Cathy and schedule a meeting. We wanted to meet Cathy. Cathy agreed to meet. We met at Cathy's home where her office was set up. Oops….another red flag was going up! Cathy's large home was beautifully decorated. Her husband greeted us at the door and led us to Cathy's office. Cathy sat on her side of the massive desk and we sat on the other. She started to explain about how she had helped mom with life insurance paperwork after dad's death, moms will and moms banking. She had even taken deposits to the bank on mom's behalf. My sister spoke up about the will. Cathy stated that since both of us lived out of state that neither Ann nor I could not be the executrix. We told her that was not correct. Anyone, no matter where they lived could be an executrix according to the law. She said that was not true. In other words, she lied to us. We just wanted to hear those words out of her mouth. There was a few minutes of chit chat and we suggested to mom that we needed to go.

Later that night we sat down and told mom how Cathy was wrong about the will and that she could have either one of us as executrix to her will. We barely knew this woman and we both walked away feeling we couldn't trust her. Mom continued to tell us Cathy knew what she was talking about and that we were the ones that are wrong.

The next day it was time for my sister and me to head home. We begged mom to rethink the will. We suggested she call the attorney Jake that was a friend of my dad's. She said no and that Cathy and Jake work together in matters concerning wills. Yet another red flag was going up. I thought my head would explode.

Whenever we talked to mom she always talked about Cathy. Cathy had "made friends" with other residents in the retirement community as well. She seemed to befriend residents whose family members lived out of state....just like my mom's! Another red flag! We tried so many times to get mom to look for another Certified Financial Planner and see if they agreed with Cathy's plan. Mom told us no and she believed in Cathy and her plan. Mom felt that since Cathy was a Certified Financial Planner and an ordained minister she believed what was said.

For several days I had tried to call mom. There was no answer. I had called my sister and told her I had not talked to her in a few days. She said the same thing. We thought maybe she was grocery shopping, getting her hair done or socializing. A few days later neither one of us had been able to talk to her. This was really strange. Her days were pretty much all the same with the exception of an outing with other residents. Ann called the retirement community and spoke with the receptionist, Maggie. Maggie remembered my sister as she had spent a lot of time with mom and dad during a visit in the fall before dad died. She hesitated, sighed and told Ann that she wasn't supposed to tell us. Tell us what? Maggie told Ann that she was in the hospital. Ann thanked her for the information. Yet another red flag!

My sister decided she'd call the hospital to see if mom was a patient there. Low and behold, she was. The call got transferred to mom's room. My sister had a conversation with mom while she was in the hospital and said that we were really worried about her and we both had tried to call her every day. She said she didn't want us to worry about her and Cathy was taking care of everything and Cathy also told mom she didn't need to tell Ann and me that she was in the hospital. Yet another red flag! Later in the days that followed we found out just how Cathy really took care of our mother. Cathy had handled all of mom's banking. She even got mom to sign a power of attorney to get into my mom's bank account. Cathy's deceptive acts were getting far worse than what we knew. Mom had given her power of attorney. Ann and I felt helpless as we both felt our mother was being taken advantage of by this wretched woman!

The next day I received a call from one of her doctors at the hospital. He told me that mom had coded but they had brought her back. She had been having problems with her heart. I asked if I needed to come up right then and explained I lived four hours away. He said no, not yet. When we hung up, it was the "not yet" part I couldn't understand. My head was whirling with "what ifs". I wanted to be with her. Something very serious was going on. I called John. John adored my parents and lived nearby.

John and I were married for many years and he is the father of my two children Ben and Adam. John and my parents were very close. Some may say he was closer to my parents than he was with his own and my parents loved him. He was considered a son to them.

When I talked to John he said he would go by the hospital and check on her then call me to let me know what was going on. It was right after this call that I received a second call from the doctor and said that mom had coded again and that I should come to the hospital. I said I was on my way and to tell my mom that I love her. I hung up the phone. My mind was reeling and my stomach was tied up in knots. This couldn't be happening. I called William and told him what was going on and to meet me at home to pack some clothes so we could get on the road to Virginia. I don't remember driving home. I don't even remember throwing clothes into my bag. I asked William if I should pack funeral clothes. He said not to worry about that right now. If we needed funeral clothes we would get them in Virginia. William is always my voice of logic and reason. We were in the car and headed out of town when we received a call from John. When I answered the call I knew from the sound of his voice that things were not good. Since

I was driving, I pulled over. He simply said "she's gone". I was devastated. I told him we had just started our drive to Virginia and it would be about four hours until we got to the hospital. He told me to take our time and that he would stay with mom until we got there.

William told me to switch seats and he would drive. I remember sitting in the passenger's seat very quietly but my mind was once again whirling. How could this be? Why we were not told she was in the hospital earlier, we could have been there! How had she died? I immediately called my sister Ann. I told her what I knew and that John was staying at the hospital until we got there. Since my sister just had shoulder surgery she was unable to make the trip. To make things a little worse, William got pulled over for speeding. William explained to the state trooper that we were on our way to Virginia because my mom had just died. I'm assuming the state trooper had no compassion whatsoever to our situation and gave William a speeding ticket even though he could see how physically upset I was. Great…just what we need.

We finally got to the hospital and found our way to mom's room. John was there waiting on us. It was quite obvious he had been there quite some time. He looked at me with tears in his eyes and said how sorry he was and how much he loved my mom. I remember him hugging me. I reached down and looked at mom. She looked so beautiful and at peace. Her arms were cold. William held my hand. She truly was gone. I thanked John for staying as long as he did. He wanted to give William and me time alone. Looking back, I don't know how many people, especially an ex-husband would do what John did and how understanding his wife was. I always knew he loved my mom. The room was very quiet and peaceful. The nurses commented what a really great patient she was and how happy she seemed. Mom must have known that this was how she wanted to die…quietly, peacefully and happy. But I never got the opportunity to tell her I loved her or hold her hand just one more time.

William and I checked into a hotel. I called my sister. We discussed having a memorial service and we both knew mom wanted to be cremated. Since Ann was unable to make a trip to Virginia we would try and postpone the memorial service about two weeks.

The next day we went to the retirement home where my mother lived. The receptionist was very kind to us and told us how sorry she was to hear about my mother. I told her I had a key to mom's apartment and we were going up there. We pushed the button for the elevator to go to the second floor.

My mother had always told me that if anything ever happened to her to "get the green box". This box was metal and had a lock on it. She even told me where the box was located in her apartment. She said the wills, account numbers and other important papers are in this green box. I unlocked mom's apartment door and William and I walked in. The place looked tidy and clean. I headed straight to the green box. We were going to take this box straight to the bank and let them know mom just died and get some guidance. I picked up the green box, locked the apartment up and headed to the elevator to get to the lobby. William and I stepped off the elevator and heard someone shouting "stop right there". We looked up and saw Cathy running towards us waiving some papers. Again, she said "stop right there". I remember William and I looking at each other and wondering what was going on. Since William had never met Cathy, I looked over to him and told him that was Cathy. Cathy stopped in front of us and asked what we were doing with the box. I told her we were going to the bank since this is what mom had always told me to do. She shouted out "I'm the executrix of your mother's estate. I need to take an inventory of what is in that box". I remember saying "like Hell you are". The papers she had in her proved her right. I looked at William and told him I couldn't believe this and pulled out my cell phone to call my sister. The more Cathy talked, the louder she got. It was quite embarrassing. I walked outside to call my sister. Ann and I couldn't believe mom actually made Cathy executrix. We knew Cathy was deceitful but this took deceit to a whole new level. How dare this ordained minister and Certified Financial Planner tell such lies to our mother only to make money from my mother's death! How dare she! We later found out that my mother wasn't the only one in that retirement home that this happened to.

Cathy told us to go to the craft room so she could inventory the contents of the green box. I told her no and that I was going to the bank. She said she would go with us. I let her inventory what was in the green box. Of course mom's will was in there which had been changed so Cathy would be executrix. There was also important account numbers, a coin collection, dad's wallet, keys to the deposit box and stock certificates. Cathy wanted to know if the coins were valued at face value or if they were rare. I took them and said I would find out. She made me sign for them and wanted me to take them to a dealer to find out their worth and get a letter stating if they were worth face value or rare coins. I gave her the stink eye and took them. I was seething! I'd handle this when I got home. Everything was placed back in the green box and we went to the bank. Once inside the bank, Cathy steam rolled over us to get to the bank manager. I wanted to find out about the safety deposit box. Only Cathy could get the contents of the deposit box. I was furious. It's a good thing William was there to calm me down. My parents worked very hard all their lives and saved what they could over the course of their marriage. And now I felt like Cathy was invading very personal matters that my parents worked for all their lives. She had no rights!

William and I left the bank and made a visit to the funeral home. We told them about my mom's wishes to be cremated and a memorial service would be sometime in the very near future since my sister was unable to travel from New York because of her recent surgery. It was so refreshing to be in a calm and peaceful funeral home. The staff was very compassionate. We scheduled the memorial service several weeks later so my sister could come down. Still, in the back of my mind, I was seething about everything Cathy had done.

William and I went back to the retirement community and requested a meeting with the administrator Linda. We wanted to tell her about mom's arrangements and getting her apartment cleaned out. Linda met with us with a hint of hesitation. She looked as though something was on her mind. She didn't make eye contact with me and she seemed terribly nervous. I thought it was very strange but everything seemed strange to me at that time.

We walked into her office and she said how terribly sorry she was about my mother's passing. She told us how much she loved our mother and how much she made everyone laugh. And then she started fidgeting. I knew something was wrong. Linda explained that the executive staff had a meeting about my mother while she was in the hospital. She explained that when the paramedics came to get my mother that she had them stop at the front desk. My mother handed the receptionist a note. The note said that mom did not want them to contact her daughters because she did not want them to worry about her. She further stated that a few days later my mother's health was deteriorating. It was at that time the executive committee, which included Cathy, had decided they should contact my sister and me. Cathy said she would contact us about our mother and let us know our mothers condition.

My sister nor I ever received a call from Cathy. Why didn't she call? This wretched woman kept us from seeing our mother. This wretched woman kept us from saying our last good byes. This wretched woman kept us from knowing our mothers true condition. Why? I now know it was because of the despicable things she did in regards of my mother's financial matters. She had gone behind our backs and had mom give her access to her bank accounts by getting mom to make her power of attorney and make her executor of her will. I stood up, I tried to compose myself and said "how could you do this"? "You are the Director of this facility. How could you let this happened". Linda began to cry. She knew how horrible this was. Maybe she knew in the back of her mind she would get sued? I was so angry and visibly shaken. This was my mother! We left the room and went outside. I was broken hearted and cried. I cried hard.

Once I got myself together I called my sister and told her what happened. My sister was shocked. Since she had just undergone her shoulder surgery she had to wait two weeks before her doctor would allow her to travel.

Two weeks later my sister was able to make the drive from upstate New York to Virginia. The memorial service was scheduled several days after she arrived and was a beautiful celebration of mom's life. We had lots of pictures of mom and dad, my sister and I, our children and grandchildren. Family had come from New York and Florida. The retirement community brought residents on the bus to the service. Immediately after the service we had a reception line to greet everyone. My sister and I were standing next together. At the very same moment, my sister and I felt something strange. We both looked up and Cathy comes through the doors with some papers in her hand. She comes up to us and says she needed our signature on some documents. We couldn't believe she had the audacity to ask us to sign papers right there at our mother's memorial service. It was at that moment my cousin Dennis and William heard what she was saying to my sister and me. Both of them stepped up and told her "no, we were not signing anything here" and that she needed to leave immediately. How does someone think that signing paperwork at a memorial service is right to begin with? First, you would be signing some kind of legal document under duress. Second, it's downright rude to come to a funeral where you're not wanted.

During the next several days, we all cleaned out mom's apartment. One of the first things my sister and I did was to search for any information mom may have kept concerning our adoption. We did not find anything. Linda had come up to mom's apartment and got furious about us cleaning out the apartment. We had told her that she had been notified several weeks ago and she had agreed. Apparently she had forgotten. She even threatened to call the police. We calmly explained that she had given us permission before and that since we were all from out of state that it would be best for us to take care of it now rather than come back at a later date.

My purpose of telling this sad story is to serve as a warning to you. If you have a loved one in a retirement community be aware especially if you live in another state. Check in with them every day. Find out who calls them. Find out who they talk to. Most importantly, find out who comes to visit them. If you have an uneasy feeling, dig your heels in and talk to the administrators. It is the responsibility of administrators and staff to keep residents safe. We are confident that Linda and Cathy were in on some type of sick scam. After consulting with an attorney, we could have prosecuted but decided not to. We had a solid case but it would have cost us tens of thousands of dollars to do anything about it. Even the attorney cried when we told her the story. Elderly citizens are easily preyed upon and made victims by people they deem "reliable". Be very aware. Protect your loved ones.

Chapter 3

THE BIRTH OF A NEW
GENERATION

IT SEEMED LIKE the next few years flew by after my parent's death. I missed them both so much. When I had a tough day at work or when I just wanted to hear her voice and laugh I would start to pick up the phone, only to realize she wouldn't be there. In conversations with my sister she told me she would often listen to a saved voicemail on her phone just to hear her voice for comfort. I felt like an orphan all over again. I had no parents. They were gone. At times, the loss and grief was almost unbearable.

Things were beginning to get brighter. Both of my sons were expecting their first child at about the same time. I was thrilled to be G-ma times TWO! I could hardly wait. Ben's child was due mid-December and Adam's child was due the first of January.

I was traveling to Southwest, Virginia to attend Adam and Amanda's gender reveal party. I had never been to a gender reveal party before and I could hardly wait to see if I would have a grandson or a granddaughter. All I wanted was for both of my sons to have healthy babies. As I was driving, my oldest son Ben called me. When I answered he was so excited he could hardly contain himself. He told me they were expecting a baby girl. I was thrilled beyond words. All I could think about was buying pink princess dresses, pink shoes, pink blankets, pink everything. Everyone was healthy and Baby girl was due in December. I remember how truly blessed I felt. God was giving me a granddaughter.

I pulled into the driveway of Adam and Amanda's house. Their home was filled with friends anxious to find out if Amanda would have a boy or girl. Adam gathered everyone outside to the backyard. He had set up a board with about 30 balloons attached with a message inside. Each person was given a dart. One balloon had the gender of the baby inside. One by one, each person took their turn at throwing a dart at a balloon in hopes of popping the balloon that would reveal the gender of the baby. I could feel my heart racing with anticipation. I already learned earlier in the day that I was having one granddaughter, what was this child going to be? All the balloons were popped. None of them revealed the gender. Wait! I could tell by the look on Adam and Amanda's face something was up. Adam has always been a prankster. Adam disappeared. Moments later he returned with yet another board with six more balloons. He jokingly said the first board was just for us to practice. Of course we all laughed. He asked who wanted to go next. I volunteered. I took the dart in my hand. I took careful aim, drew back my arm and the dart went through the air and popped a balloon. A message floated to the ground. Adam picked it up and read it. He announced "It's a girl". Everyone was so excited. I started hugging Amanda and Adam. I later found out that Adam and Amanda didn't plan that I would be the one to pop the revealing message but they were glad I was the one. We were all thrilled it turned out that way. God has blessed me with two granddaughters in the same day.

Several days later it was time for me to go home. I remember thinking how much fun my parents would have had at the party. They loved to get together with family and this one would have been so much fun for them to hear they would be having two great granddaughters. I could feel my parents smiling down on me. I'm very certain they were looking down and enjoying every minute of the festivities.

Waiting for the birth of a child can seem like an eternity. The closer it got to December the more anxious I would become awaiting the birth of my first granddaughter. Every time the phone would ring I'd jump.

Finally, the big day arrives. Ben calls me and tells me they're in the hospital. It's time! I already had my suitcase packed and ready to go. I tell William it's time, Sarah is in the hospital. William was unable to go with me. Next thing I know I'm on my way back to Virginia to meet my granddaughter. This is it! It's finally happening. Baby girl, your mee-maw is on her way. I don't remember much about the drive to Virginia, but I do remember praying for a healthy baby. I remember praying for mercy on Sarah. I remember praying for the doctors, the nurses and especially for my granddaughter. This was a monumental day in our lives.

By the time I got there my granddaughter made her entrance into this world. Sarah was sitting up in bed holding their precious daughter. They had named her Laura. Laura was so tiny. Her cheeks were chubby. She reminded me of a sweet little cherub. Thank you God for this beautiful healthy girl. Ben was so proud. Sarah handed the baby to Ben, he introduced me to his daughter and handed her to me. I couldn't believe how beautiful she was. She was perfect. I sat down and held this dear child for quite some time. I didn't want to let her go. I imagined all the fun things we would do together like tea parties with her favorite stuffed animals, playing princess dress up, making cookies and shopping. I whispered in her ear that I was her grandma and that I loved her to the moon and back. A nurse came in to take her back to the nursery. Mommy and Daddy both looked tired. I told them I was going to check into a hotel and be back in the morning.

The next day I came back to the hospital. My precious granddaughter was waiting for me. I swear she smiled at me when I picked her up from her bassinet. Mom and dad seemed to be doing OK. It looked like they had gotten some rest. I remember taking Ben down to the cafeteria to get something to eat and he told me how excited he was to be a dad. I was so proud of him.

We went back upstairs. Baby Laura was fast asleep. Other family members had come to meet the newest addition. I had to say goodbye to my sweet granddaughter and go back to North Carolina. Tears rolled down my face. This was tough, but I knew I'd be back as soon as I could.

The next couple of weeks flew by. Christmas came and went and the New Year rolled in. It was less than a week after New Year's I get a call from Adam. It was time for their precious daughter to make her entrance into the world.

I packed my bags and headed back to Virginia. After a five hour trip, I got to meet sweet Ella. She had a head full of dark hair and beautiful brown eyes. When I finally got my turn at holding her for the first time I couldn't help but wonder about all the good things she could be in this world. Again, I whispered in her ear that I was her grandma and I couldn't wait to have a tea party with her and her favorite stuffed animals, and how much fun we'd have baking her favorite cookies, shopping and playing together. Now I have two beautiful granddaughters. God has really blessed this family once again.

Fast forward several years, Amanda and Adam blessed our family with a grandson. His name is Paul Wesley, named after his great grandfather. All three of these grand children have brought me great joy. They're personalities are so different. Their hearts are pure and full of love.

Both Ben and Adam would call me after they took their children to doctor's appointment and tell me how they went. Several times they would ask me if I knew anything about my health background. Because I was adopted, there was so many unknown factors concerning my health which my granddaughters may have inherited. It was the birth of my two granddaughters and grandson that I thought it was time to delve into finding my biological family for this very reason.

Chapter 4

───❧───

THINGS TO CONSIDER BEFORE BEGINNING YOUR JOURNEY

MORE THAN 20 million people have had their DNA sequenced. 10 million of those tests happened since 2016. In November, 2018 from Thanksgiving to Cyber Monday, Ancestry.com had record breaking sales. There are many testing companies consumers can choose such as Ancestry.com, 23andMe, My Heritage and Family Tree. The list goes on and on. The DNA testing kit you choose depends on what information you are looking for. DNA testing is the main source of information for adoptees.

Your search will be an emotional roller coaster that should be carried out with respect. You may find stories surrounding your birth that may have mysteries, lies, cover ups, guilt and shame. Or, you could come across biological parents that have been waiting for you to find them. You may also discover one or both of your biological parents are deceased. Throughout my travels, I have heard many stories that are truly uplifting and others that just break my heart into a million pieces. I've been on this roller coaster ride too and I find my faith in God has helped. I find my hope for the future generations of my family that they will have answers too. And perseverance pays off. You have a right to know who you are. You have the right to know where you come from. Once you have answers, no matter if they're positive or negative, you can move forward in your life.

Completing a DNA testing kit can be fun and give you lots of information. You will find out where your descendants came from, a health profile and find family member matches. Understand that your test will give you the whole story. Don't think the test should be used to diagnose a condition or medical management. Just because the test may reveal you are prone to cancer or Alzheimer's doesn't mean you will develop the disease. Fortunately in my case, the medical information I received from my DNA test basically pointed to coming from a long line of healthy "stock". I later found out it is true.

In my travels, I have heard many remarkable stories where someone found out that the person that raised them as their mother was really their grandmother. Some learned that their aunt is really their sister or that their uncle was really their father. And some found out they have a half sibling from a past relationship their parent had. We must first remember our biological parents are human beings. We all make mistakes, mistakes some wish to cover up. But it happens. It's part of life. You never know who may pop up as a relative. For me, the more family that pops up, the merrier. I have a lot of love in my heart for more family.

From my experience, finding relatives has been a wonderful thing. Be aware that not everyone feels the same way I do. Some have said they wished they had never decided to take a DNA test because of the relatives they have met as a result of their matches. Their relative had turned out to be a fraud and was seeking money from them. That's despicable but it does happen.

Here's a few things to consider before you spit or swab a sample of your DNA and send it off:

- Be prepared, you may be a deep dark family secret.
- What if you have always believed you were a natural born child to your parents only to find out you're adopted?
- What if you were a product of artificial insemination or a sperm donor?
- What if you were expecting one outcome only to find out otherwise? Are you willing to be able to cope with the mental stress of this?
- Are you going to be able to handle a close match that chooses not to communicate with you?
- Your information will remain in the DNA's company database indefinitely. Be prepared and know that years later a new close match may pop up.
- Don't be disappointed if you meet new relatives and you don't like them.
- You share DNA with your relatives. If you choose to take a DNA test remember you are providing information about them too.

Chapter 5

INSTRUCTION GUIDE FOR
BEING WITH AN ADOPTEE

ADOPTEES CAN BE a mixed bag of nuts. We tend to be "pleasers". If we are not pleasing others, we may have a fear of being sent away. Adoptees may also have a fear of loss for something that they don't even have a clue they have lost. There are seven core issues adoptees face. Some adoptees may not have all seven so I will go forth in this chapter from my point of view. So readers, buckle up!

Loss and Grief: These are little words that mean big things. Since I was five days old when I was adopted, it's not really clear whether I have memories of my birth mother and father. The day I was placed in my adoptive parents arms must have been a magical day for them. As I grew older, it seemed to be some kind of pull back to another time. I felt loss for something I never understood. How could this be? I was a happy child. Why did I feel like this? My identity issues were starting to surface about the age of 13. My loss became quite evident when we moved from upstate New York to Virginia in the late 60's. I felt jerked out of all my surroundings I had grown up with. I felt a tremendous amount of loss; loss of friends, loss of family, loss of home and loss of the surroundings I loved and felt secure in. Before we moved, we lost our dog Patsy and now I have to start high school in a different school. To this 13 year old girl it was devastating.

Rejection and Abandonment: Somewhere deep down I knew my biological mother "relinquished" me out of love for my best interests. But it's still a rejection. I was given up! Given up for what? I felt rejected and left out in elementary school. The other children would laugh at me and make fun of me because I was adopted. The only place I felt some semblance of belonging was in Girl Scouts. Maybe because my adoptive mom was the troop leader. When we moved to Virginia, I felt so alone in my new school. I hated school. Some girls in school tried to become my friend but I pushed them away. I told them there was no point in being friends. I would only be here two years then go back home to graduate with my friends in New York and I would be out of this hell hole. That never happened. It must have been about half way through my sophomore year I had an epiphany. We were not going back to New York and I would be graduating from high school in Virginia. Some may view this as eccentric or exaggerated but these are very real feelings that an adoptee may experience. And WOW…do they start early in life!

Guilt and Shame: Here's a quote from Brooke Randolph, Licensed Medical Health Counselor written June 24, 2014 that personally sums me up. "Enduring feelings of guilt may lead to the experience of guilt even in inappropriate situations. Some who have been adopted into greater means have felt guilt that their birth/first family has not had the same opportunity and may be living in poverty. In some situations, adoptees may try to give away possessions or large sums of money."

In school, I was always giving away note paper, pencils or money for lunch. That was because I had it and the person I was giving it to was truly in need. I felt guilty that I had something they needed. It seemed natural for me to just give it to them. It seemed like second nature to me. I always thought it was a good thing to do…helping others. My husband and I have even given away two storage units of furniture away to others in need. Giving always makes my heart happy and I always feel good about it deep down inside. Maybe this is a part of my nature always wanting to be "the good girl". If I continued to do good things, I would be wanted, I would be loved and I wouldn't be let go again. Later I would learn there was economic differences in my biological parents and my adoptive parents.

Identity: As an adoptee, the question that seems to be constant was "where do I fit in?" I would be at the dinner table looking at my sister, mom and dad and think that I didn't look anything like any of them. It felt odd. My sister's hair was dark and really curly. I remember having to iron her hair back in the 60's. Yup, we really did that. My hair was a lighter brown and straight as a stick. I didn't have any of my parent's facial features. Who do I look like? Do I have the same eyes as any of my biological family? Do I have any of the same mannerisms? Maybe I would be able to find out somehow. Does my biological family have the same religious beliefs as I do? Maybe someday I will go searching for my family. In my late teens, I knew one thing for sure. I am who I am. I fought everyday not to cave to peer pressure in my late teens because I didn't want to be rejected yet again. God has put me on this earth for a greater good. I didn't know what it was then, but one thing for sure my dear reader is I am certain of what my greater good is now and I strive to always work towards that greater good.

Intimacy: Somewhere at the age of about the mid 20's to mid-30's an adoptees brain is developed enough to understand the complexity and impact it has on their lives. Identity and fear of being rejected or abandoned may contribute to intimacy difficulties. It may even be a reason why adoptees will hesitate to find biological family because they may be rejected again.

Control: As adoptees, we were not asked to be given away. For this reason, adoptees often feel the need to be in control. Speaking for myself, I find this to be very true. I'm a planner and a micro-manager. I thrive on making sure details are correct. I don't like it but I'm sure I am. This issue of control is one I am working on by not stressing and "letting go". I've come a long way to trusting people in performing tasks. In other words, I'm trying not to sweat the small stuff.

Fear: To me, fear is so traumatic. I'm in fear of losing a loved one. I'm in fear of being rejected. I'm in fear of not being good enough. To some, these fears may seem ridiculous but it's a battle every day and I'm working on it. It seems that the older I get it somehow gets easier to deal with. After much thought, I believe some of these fears are unfounded since finding my biological family and the love they have shown me.

Chapter 6

TAKING THE DNA PLUNGE

IT HAS BEEN over five years now since I took the DNA plunge. William and I were watching television one evening and a commercial for a DNA testing kit came on. The first time I saw it I hardly paid any attention to it. The second time I saw it I paid more attention to it. The third time I saw the commercial I googled it to find out more. What was this DNA kit all about? How did it work? What could I expect from the results? This particular test was 23andMe.com. They claimed that they could tell you where you came from, your ethnicity, match you to relatives and health information. WHAT? Who knew! At this time the kit was $199 plus shipping. I talked to William about it and we decided to give it a try.

I ordered my DNA kit and received it in the mail. I opened it up and read the directions. One of the first things they tell you to do is to be sure to register your kit number online. So I did. The next step was to get my saliva into a tube that had a cap on it. To be honest, spitting into this tube was not fun. It took me awhile to fill it up to the line marked on the side of the tube. After the tube was filled, I snapped the tube shut and mailed it back to the company. The instructions said it would take six to eight weeks to process and that I would receive an email when my results were ready. So I waited…..and waited….and waited!

I tried to put the waiting and anticipation out of my mind by keeping busy. I think I must have checked my email ten times a day. Finally the day came and I received my email from 23andMe. I pray I would have medical information for Ben and Adam. I prayed for my grandchildren. And I prayed I have biological matches. I logged into my account. I found out that I am primarily from Great Britain, Wales and Ireland. There was a fascinating chart showing the migration of my ancestors that come from Europe and landed in upstate New York. According to the information, my ancestors had fled Europe because of the potato famine. This was all so fascinating to me. I had no idea. I then clicked on my health statistics. It showed that I liked coffee and chocolate, which is very true. It continued to state that I was less likely to have dementia and Alzheimer's, heart disease, cancer, lung issues and we have a history of longevity. Basically I came from a long line of very healthy ancestors.

The time had come to click on the DNA matches tab. This is it. This is what I've been waiting for. I was finally going to find out who my biological family is! After a half century of wondering, asking questions that would never get answered, and the spit in the tube was going to answer all my questions. YES! Without further anticipation, I clicked the tab!

The DNA matches were listed in order by closest matches first. I had thousands of distant cousin matches. My closest match was a female second cousin with a name I did not recognize. I scanned down to see if there were any names I recognized and there were none. I knew it would be a long-shot but I thought I'd give it a try. I had several third and fourth matches. So now what? I certainly didn't understand all this new lingo since I just don't seem to have a scientific gene in my DNA makeup. I must admit I was somewhat disappointed since I was hoping for something a little closer. I logged out and decided to think about this and do a little research and hope to get enough nerve to reach out to a few of my matches.

I talked it over with William as to what to possibly write in a message. We talked out several different scenarios. This could be life changing not only for myself but to the person I was reaching out to. Was I a family secret? Or, could this be the correspondence my match had always been waiting for? There's one thing you should know when you attempt to reach out in a situation like this. Be prepared for any outcome. Emails may not be returned. Phone calls may not be returned. Letters sent in the mail may never be answered. It's a roll of the dice. As Dory from the movie Finding Nemo would say while she was looking for her family "*just keep swimming, swimming, swimming.*"

About a week later I decided to start reaching out. Nothing ventured, nothing gained. In 23andMe.com, you can see when matches last logged in. Several of the matches I had, had not logged in many months, even years. I chose to reach out to a woman named Joyce. After relentlessly looking through Facebook, I began to learn a little about her. She was married, loves her dogs and birds, seems to like the arts, and lives in Tampa, Florida. She was a strong third to fourth cousin and I found us to look somewhat alike. We are even the same age. I thought it best to keep the email short but to the point. I simply explained that I was an adoptee from upstate New York and was looking for my biological family and would she be able to help me and give me information. The next thing I know she sends me information back. She was excited that I had written to her. We exchanged emails back and forth for several months and later decided to call each other. It was difficult for us to figure out how we were related. One thing we did know is that we were related but not sure if it was maternal or paternal. DNA doesn't lie! Our relationship grew to help each other out and solve this big mystery. We are both somewhat planners and we'd schedule our phone calls on Sundays. Our phone conversations went on for many months. It was sometime later that we decided to meet.

This was just the beginning. We were both about to meet biological family for the first time. I'm sure you can only imagine how thrilling it was. We just needed to work out the details.

Let me tell you what kind of amazing husband William is. William knew how excited I was after each phone conversation Joyce and I would have. I would tell him how each conversation was and how many things Joyce and I had in common. Joyce grew up in Pennsylvania and I grew up in upstate New York. We would go back to the trying to figure out what was going on in the country in the 50's to figure out the connection. Nothing seemed to come together. We still had missing pieces of the puzzle. William and I started to work out the details of me flying to Florida. This was going to be exciting!

I booked a flight to Florida in June, 2017 and arrived at the airport. It was good to be back since I had lived there some time ago. I walked out of the terminal and immediately felt the heat and humidity. YIKES! I had almost forgotten how hot it really is there.

The next day was THE day I was to finally meet Joyce, a biological family member. I was both calm and nervous all at the same time. I'm not sure if that's possible but that's the way I felt. We were going to meet at a restaurant for lunch. I made sure to look as good as I possibly could despite the heat and humidity. Since the traffic in Tampa is horrible, I knew I should leave a little early. I decided to stop by and pick up a small gift. It needed to be something to mark this very special day. It needed to be something Joyce would love. A bottle of wine? I decided no. What if she doesn't drink alcohol? What if I get red and she likes white? Then I rounded the corner in the store and saw the perfect gift! It was a Peace Lily. I knew this would be the perfect gift. Its leaves were shiny, there was new growth and it had a beautiful ribbon tied around the pot. I paid for the plant and drove to the restaurant. I walked in with the Peace Lily in hand. Now I was getting nervous. This is it! I'm meeting a true, living, breathing, biological family member. The hostess commented how beautiful the plant was. I explained it was for a cousin I was about to meet for the very first time. She brought me around the corner and said to me "there's your cousin. She's waiting for you". Joyce had told the hostess that she was meeting her cousin for the first time. All I could see was the back of Joyce's head. She had beautiful blond hair cut in a very attractive bob style. I walked over to her and said "Joyce, it's me". As you can imagine, there were many tears… happy tears. I gave her the Peace Lily and she said she was just looking at them the other day and wanted to put some around her pool. She loved it.

I can't even tell you what I had for lunch that day. That is kind of a blur. But I can tell you how amazingly comfortable I felt talking to her. It seemed like we were on the same page. She looks like me. She's got a sense of humor like me and had the same color eyes as me. Her mannerisms were just like me. She is tall like me. I chuckled to myself that she was thinner than me. We talked for hours about growing up, our parents and places we had been. Joyce is amazing! We both felt relaxed. We talked and laughed for hours. Joyce invited me to come to her house for dinner the next day and meet her husband and a cousin of hers that would be celebrating a birthday. I was thrilled. Since it was a birthday and I'm a planner, I needed to come up with another cool idea yet another family member I hadn't met yet.

On the drive back, I went to a party store. Since it was a birthday for a very special someone in Joyce's life and a cousin I hadn't met yet, I better come up with something fun. I found tiaras, party beads and noise makers and stuffed them into a gift bag for everyone. I'm not one to go to someone's house empty handed.

The next day I arrived at Joyce's home. Her home should be in a magazine. It was stunning. Her husband was making dinner and the aroma coming out of the kitchen was to die for. It was salmon and authentic German potato salad. I met Betty, the birthday girl and Eric, Joyce's husband and chef. Betty is in her 90's and she's so sweet and spunky. She couldn't figure out how were related but if DNA testing said we were, then we were. I presented everyone with a gift bag and we all sat around talking until dinner was ready. I met all of Joyce's fur babies which included a cockatoo, several canaries, and two whippets. Joyce took me out to the back of the house where there was a pool with beautiful landscaping and the Peace Lily. All this was overlooking a lake. It was like a picture perfect postcard.

Dinner was served. I don't think I have ever had salmon that was as good as Eric had made. The authentic German potato salad was warm and delicious. As I was sitting at the table, I became overwhelmed. Tears were running down my face. I was sitting at a dinner table with family, family that looked like me. This was something I had always dreamed of. God is good!

We all celebrated Betty's birthday with cake and gifts. It was getting late and time for me to go. I was heading back home the next day. I didn't want to leave. This is my family.

As I boarded the plane the next day, I realized how blessed I am. Some may say, well…she's just a fourth cousin. What's the big deal? Let me tell you my friend…it's a big deal. It's family.

Chapter 7

———∕∾∿∾∖———

My Angel's Name is Carol

SINCE I ACTUALLY met a biological family member, it had made me more determined to find my biological parents and any biological siblings. I had prayed to God for answers. It was at this time God led me to a solution that would change everything. I needed to enlist the help of a search angel.

What is a "search angel"? A search angel is a person that volunteers their time and resources to help adoptees find biological family. Search angels know what you are going through and can guide you through your search and what to do when you find biological family. Many help out of the kindness of their hearts and never ask for payment. Search angels have ways of accessing information you would never possibly dream of. The DNA information from your test kit will give them many clues even if your biological family has not taken one.

Do you keep coming up with road blocks in your search? Consider finding a search angel. Search angels can be found on Facebook pages that are dedicated to adoptees searching for biological family. Other sources are adoption registries and adoption.com. Once a search angel has agreed to help you, be sure to give them all the information you have. Don't leave out anything. My search angel suggested I get my non-identifying information and take an Ancestry.com test in addition to the 23andMe.com test I had already taken.

Before you choose to work with a search angel, be cautious. You may want to consider getting a background check done. Be sure to get references. Remember, you do not know them well and you will be giving them very personal information.

My trip to Florida to meet Joyce was amazing to say the least. I was still checking my 23andMe.com matches every day. Sometimes I would check it five or six times a day. I would continue to reach out to matches and found little or no results in responses. During this time, DNA companies were doing a lot of advertising. It seemed the most popular testing companies were 23andMe.com and Ancestry.com. It was at this point I was trying to determine if I should take an Ancestry.com DNA test to see if the matches would be different. If I'm not getting responses from my 23andMe.com matches, would I have better luck with Ancestry.com? I felt stuck. I believed the more people that took DNA tests, the more chances I would have more matches.

I kept seeing several different adoptee search groups on Facebook. I joined them, read their posts and hoped to learn some new things that would help me with my search. One day I decided to "go fishing" on one of the DNA groups. I posted my frustrations with trying to understanding the "lingo" of everything DNA. In my post I also included a little information about myself and where things stood in my search. Within minutes I get a reply. "I think I can help you." Someone by the name of Carol took the bait. She explained to me that she was a genealogy researcher and had been connecting adoptees like myself for over twenty years. I gave her my log in information on 23andMe so she could take a look at what information I had. She would call me back later after reviewing the information. It took a few weeks before I spoke with her. At this point my closest match was a male third cousin. I explained to Carol that I had researched his information the best I could and found his address. I sent him a letter but never got any response. It's really frustrating to get no response.

Carol had delved into my DNA vigorously. She explained to me she had found the daughter of my third cousin. Since my third cousin is an older gentleman, he may have been shocked getting my letter. We talked about contacting his daughter to see if she could offer any further insights. Carol made the call to my third cousin's daughter. The daughter explained that he did get the letter and thought it was a scam. Carol told her it wasn't and that I was really the person I said I was and looking for my biological family. The daughter was on board and gave Carol what little information she knew about the family. Later we would learn the information was somewhat helpful but there were still missing pieces of the puzzle. I understand how an older person would think a letter such as mine would have been a scam since he had moved from upstate New York to Florida to retire and enjoy a quieter and simpler life. He thought I was after his money. All I wanted was to find out any family information that would lead me to closer matches.

Carol and I had decided to further my search by doing two things. The first would be to do an Ancestry.com DNA test. This would give us more clues and matches and we would be closer to finding my biological family. It was time to open Pandora's Box and see just what's inside. At this time it was the most popular method for adoptees looking for biological family. The second would be to get my non-identifying information for the New York State Health Department, which I did. I ordered my Ancestry kit and while I was waiting for my test to arrive in the mail, I printed off the forms for non-identifying information from New York State. I filled out the forms, got them notarized and sent them off in the mail. Now it's another waiting game.

I received my Ancestry DNA information first. The Ancestry test showed so much more information and so many more matches. I called Carol and told her I received the results and gave her my log in information. This is where she really started digging. At one point I nick named her "Digger" since she had a way of delving into information far more than I could ever dream of.

During this time I would talk to my sister Ann about what was going on. She found it interesting. Like me, she didn't understand the lingo. We both laughed when I told her I had over 1,100 cousins. I suggested she give it try, get a DNA test and see what's out there. And she did!

Several weeks went by after Carol pilfered through my Ancestry account. When Carol would send me a message asking me to call her, I would drop everything and call her immediately. I remember one time she answered the phone and said "that was fast" and I would say "yes it was because you always have something awesome to say". On this particular day she told me she had "a mother suspect". My heart started beating so fast when I heard those words. I said "are you sure?" and she said she was pretty sure. We talked about who this person was. She was a woman that fit the age from my non-identifying information and lived in the same area I was born. She had sent me pictures of her and there was some resemblance. We had the same shape nose and big eyes. Most of the information was pegged. The suspect lived in the area where I was born and her age matched up with my non-identifying information. This could be it! We collaborated on how to reach out. I drafted a letter, emailed it to Carol, she called and said it was great. I sent the letter certified. This was the most difficult letter I had ever written. I knew I had only one opportunity to get her attention. I explained that I was working with a search angel to find my biological family and that I was adopted in New York State in 1955. The letter also included "If you are the person I have been searching for I want you to know that I thank you from the bottom of my heart for your unselfish act of giving me up for adoption. I have a truly amazing family that is full of love." A little over a week later, she had signed for the letter. And I waited, and I waited, and I waited some more for some kind of response from her. This was pure agony. She had my address and I also included my phone number in case she wanted to call me. I called Carol and told her that the suspect had received the letter. I marveled at the suspect's handwriting that was on the receipt of the certified letter. It was beautiful. Carol told me to be patient. The suspect was about 81 years old at that time and news like this could be a game changer. I expressed my empathy to Carol. What would it be like to be the suspect's age and get a letter like this in the mail? Often times, families of her era would make a decision about a single female family member having a child out of wedlock and give the baby up for adoption. It was felt that was the right thing to do. And often times the subject would never, ever be brought up again. Times like these are surely different now.

A few weeks went by and I got no response. I felt that every day that went by I was less likely I to ever hear anything. Maybe she had put my birth in the past to be forever forgotten. Maybe she was trying to figure out how to tell her family? Maybe she just didn't care. I was hopeful it would be different. I prayed she would contact me immediately and say "yes…it's me. I'm your mother." I called Carol and vented my frustrations. I could tell she had been through all this with other adoptees she has helped and would come up with a plan. Carol told me she would call her. A few days went by and she sent me a text. "Can you talk"? Of course, I have her on speed dial! Carol had called her and said she was such a lovely person. The suspect had read my letter and said it was very sweet but that she is not my mother. Carol even asked her if she had friends or other family members that had a baby at that time. Her answer was no. Carol relayed a message from her wishing me luck in my search. I'm sure you can imagine how disappointed I was. God is in control! He's got this! I kept praying for an answer. Time to move forward!

At this point it has been over a year of searching and close to starting year two. This roller coaster ride has been emotionally draining.

My feeling of loss was getting deeper and I really didn't know what I had lost. I found myself crying one minute and laughing the next. I kept praying. I needed a break. Since the holidays were approaching, I decided to give myself some time to take a breather. I talked to Carol and she thought it would be a good idea.

During this "breather" I just didn't know what to think. I felt a little sad, but I prayed. I felt defeated, but I prayed. If this suspect was not my mother then who is? Where is she? I kept reading all these wonderful stories of adoptees reuniting. These stories melted my heart. I was so happy these adoptees found what they were looking for. When would it be my turn? I prayed to be more patient. I put everything in God's hands.

My "breather" lasted about six months. The holidays came and went. I tried to keep busy. Then one day I get another text from Carol. "Can you talk?" So I called her. I assumed that since I took a "breather" that Carol would too. But NOOOOO. Carol is just so darn dedicated to helping adoptees and she wasn't giving up on THIS adoptee. During our conversation she had found another suspect that may be possible. However, she did let me know it was a stretch that she would be a good match. She told me the suspect's name and that she was deceased but there may be some clues in her obituary worth investigating. She had spent her career as a supply clerk on a military installation, married and had a son. If suspect number two was my biological mother, her son would be either my half-brother or full blood brother. He was a few years younger than me. When looking at suspect number two's pictures, I didn't see any resemblance at all. Carol told me that you can't always go by looks.

When we got off the phone I continued to look at pictures of suspect number two and decided to look on Facebook for her son. I was curious to see if there was any resemblance between him and me. I did find him on Facebook. I scoured his Facebook page. He has a beautiful wife and he's an entertainer. Ok…that's interesting! But I saw no resemblance between him and me. As the saying goes, I just wasn't feeling it! I sent him a friend request and he accepted. Later I sent him a private message asking him if I could call him. He said yes and the next day I called him. I told him I was an adoptee born in upstate New York and asked him he was related to suspect number two. He said he was not. He did say my story was fascinating and wished me luck. I sent Carol a text telling her about my findings. This time, I didn't feel as defeated as I felt with suspect number one. Maybe it's because I just wasn't feeling it. We both started laughing and said it was time to get back to the drawing board. God really does have a sense of humor.

At this time, I am almost four years into my search. Just so you know, at this stage of trying to find my biological family, Carol and I had been working together almost four years now and had developed an amazing friendship. She would often tell me that I was the toughest situation she had ever had. She wouldn't give up. Little did I know that during this time, Carol had really dug her heels into finding my biological family.

My sister Ann had taken a DNA test through Ancestry.com. Like me, she couldn't make heads or tails out of it. I took a look at her results and knowing what I had learned from Carol, she had some extremely great matches. It looked like she had a half-sister and half-brother match! Of course, I called her immediately. Ann was thrilled when I gave her the news. While I was talking to her I was stalking Facebook to see if I could find them there and help her learn more about them. Her half-sister lived about two hours away and her half-brother lived five minutes away. Can you imagine? This is wonderful news! My sister hops on Facebook and starts looking through her half-sisters Facebook page. There were many physical similarities. She loved animals. Ann sent her a friend request then sent her a private message. There was no response. Her half-brother did respond and was not interested in communicating. I felt sad for Ann. On a positive note, Ann had also learned who her biological mother was. Ann's biological mother was sixteen when Ann was born. She had been to a fraternity party, met a handsome college guy. One thing lead to another and she had gotten pregnant.

Being adopted and finding a relative and attempting to connect can be very complicated sometimes. Often times, adoptees find that some family members don't want to have a conversation or develop any kind of a relationship. For instance, you may be the key to a deep dark family secret that they had put to rest and now you have unlocked a family secret. This is one of the things you need to consider once you decide to take the DNA plunge.

Chapter 8

⚡

Reunion Etiquette

If you think searching for lost family is a roller coaster ride, wait until you "connect" with them. It's not easy. The connecting phase can go in so many directions. There are many scenarios with no written rules, no manuals, and no assurance the result you are hoping for will happen. Connecting will take on a life of its own. Be prepared and have a support system.

Think about this. Sometime ago a family's shape and dynamic has changed by the removal of someone. That someone could be the parent of its child, or the child, brothers, sisters whose grandparent's relationships are being disrupted.

When you are searching for biological family it is very important to read and learn about reconnection. Talk to other adoptees that have reconnected. Listen very carefully to their advice. You need to realize that the person you are searching for has no knowledge of you trying to find them and will not be prepared. I had rehearsed what to say on a phone conversation a million times in my head. Validate a place or event from the past that may hopefully be familiar. For example, I started out by saying where I was born. I mentioned where my father worked, where I went to school and some of my favorite places to shop. It was important to validate everything so there is no risk of thinking you may be a fraud or scam artist. If you know what hospital you were born in you may want to mention that as well. It just bolsters your credibility.

From this experience I learned to speak in a calm, normal tone and try and find a normal breathing pattern. Don't get excited and talk two octaves higher than normal. Don't speak too softly, be heard. I also learned to never assume anything because there may be much more to the story than you know. Most of all I learned to be patient because I learned from reading books about re-connection that there will be more layers to my story.

I spent some time going through Facebook to check out photos of my family. I did not send messages or friend requests. I just wanted to see if I looked like any of them. The resemblance was remarkable. I don't recommend messaging or friend requests until it is mutually agreed on until you meet face to face.

So you have confirmation that a biological family member you have been looking for is found is truly related and you are going to meet them for the first time. Do not be surprised if this takes place several years later. Be patient. Remember this is a shock to the person or persons you have finally found. It may take a few years for you to meet face to face.

THINGS TO REMEMBER WHEN RECONNECTING

- Be patient.
- Don't overwhelm them with gifts.
- Try and be understanding.
- Try not to have preconceived notions about new found family.
- Be open minded.
- Form your own opinions about each new relative you meet.
- Be realistic with expectations.

- Keep the first meeting short.
- Don't assume anything.
- Be open minded.
- Share your information how you found them if asked.
- Keep good records.
- Don't dwell on the past.
- Don't criticize.
- Don't blame yourself for the other person's life.
- Have your support system in place.
- Above all, be respectful.

Reunions come in many variations. Remember, this meeting is with a stranger. You need to remember that. Your relationship will take time to nurture and grow. Read as much as you can about reunions. Sometimes questions you may have will be answered in conversation. You should be patient. Keep the first meet short. Your second meeting will be much easier.

You are embarking on a journey of discovering your family and getting answers to questions. Take it slow. Your faith, hope and perseverance will pay off more than you can imagine.

Chapter 9

REBECCA LOUISE

REBECCA LOUISE GREW up as a happy child. She was the youngest of her five siblings and grew up in Eastern North Carolina. Rebecca Louise put the sparkle in her daddy's eyes. Growing up, Rebecca Louise's dad would come home from work for lunch and rock her. When it was time for him to go back to work little she would jump up and down on the sofa and screamed while she watched her daddy leave until she had lost sight of him. Rebecca Louise loved her daddy so much.

While growing up, Rebecca Louise felt as though she didn't fit in with her siblings. She felt different but could never figure out how or why. Rebecca Louise truly loved her siblings.

When she was 27 years old, she received a call from her two sisters asking if she would come by. They had something to tell her. They felt she was old enough and mature enough to know something. She arrived at her sister's home. They explained that their mother had put a child up for adoption before their mother had married their dad. Their aunt told her sisters years ago and they had kept it from Rebecca Louise as she was the baby in the family. Rebecca Louise's mother had never talked about it with her children, only her mother's siblings knew about the child. Rebecca Louise was told she had a brother. Her first thought was that she must find her brother. Her sisters were upset because she wanted to find her brother. They knew it would cause trouble. From that day forward for twenty nine years, Rebecca Louise's search was in full swing.

She spent the next twenty nine years looking for her brother. She checked records in the local library, checked courthouse records in different counties, talked to many people in several counties and even hired a private investigator. The search came up empty.

She was relentless in her efforts to find her brother. What was he like? Who did he look like? Was he married, did he have children? The thought of having another sibling was exciting to her.

Before Rebecca Louise's mother died, her mother developed an interest in genealogy. Her mother knew where her son was, the son she had given up for adoption and had even told her sisters where he was and he was doing fine. When Rebecca Louise's mother died, one of her sisters, Doris, took the genealogy records. In those records, her mother had proved that they were direct descendants of the Mayflower. Doris contacted the Mayflower Society to find out how to be certified that she was a true descendant of the Mayflower. The Mayflower Society contacted Doris and asked her to take a DNA test to make sure she was from the British Isles where the Mayflower was from. When Doris got her DNA results there happened to be a close family match of a half-brother. Doris tracked down the half-brother's grandson. The grandson gave Doris and her other sister Nina the half-brothers phone number. It now has been proven and certified they are descendants of the Mayflower.

Rebecca Louise and I have been friends for several years. We both have shared in one of our very first conversations that we were looking for lost family. We decided to meet at our local library to use their full version of Ancestry.com to see what, if any, information we could find on Rebecca Louise's brother. We had just typed her mother's name into the computer. Before we hit "search" Rebecca Louise's phone rang. It was her sister. Her sister asked her what she was doing and she told her she was at the library looking up information on their brother. Rebecca Louise knew from her sister's voice something was going on. She told her she would go outside and call her. This call was the one Rebecca Louise was waiting for, news of her lost brother. He had been found and her sister had talked to him. Ironically, he lived nearby. How exciting it was for me to be front row center of my friend finding her lost brother! I was thrilled for her. As the excitement grew from the conversation on the phone, I couldn't help wondering when it would be my turn to "get that call". Little did I know, but my call was about to come too.

The very next day Rebecca Louise was on her way to meet her brother and his wife. Come to find out, her brother lived only thirty minutes away and lived only 10 minutes away from where Rebecca Louise grew up. He even worked at a local television station with Rebecca Louise's sister Nina. Rebecca Louise could see how much he looked like her mother, even more so than her other siblings. Rebecca Louise told him she had been looking for him for twenty nine years. He was shocked. He didn't even know other siblings existed.

Rebecca Louise and her brother have known each other for eighteen months and have become very close. He will often tell her thanks, thanks for finding him. What a blessing to have found him after all these years. But her story doesn't end here.

Several weeks after finding her brother, Doris called Rebecca Louise and suggested to her that she too get a DNA test. So she did. When her results came back, she found another half-brother through her brother but her half-sister Doris was really a half sibling. This means they had different fathers! The father she grew up with was not her biological father. She felt lost. Her whole life was a lie and she was angry with her mother. Her mother had been with another man while married to the man that raised and loved Rebecca Louise.

Now Rebecca Louise's mission has changed. She was now looking for her biological father. In her search, she found she had three more sisters, all half-sisters. One sister was deceased, one lives in a nursing home and did not want anything to do with Rebecca Louise and one sister that she is now very close to. She also found out who her biological father was and unfortunately, he was been deceased since Rebecca Louise was twelve years old. She has now gone from five siblings to now having nine siblings.

Rebecca Louise felt that all of a sudden her four siblings that she grew up with were now half siblings. She was devastated and felt a great loss. Some may say that it really doesn't make a difference. To Rebecca Louise it does. It changes a person. It's just not the same. She feels like the black sheep of the family. Rebecca Louise feels that even though her four siblings will not admit that things are not different, that they really are. Some have become somewhat estranged. Is it because her personality is different? She has talked with people that knew her biological father. He enjoyed life, he loved to laugh and tell jokes just like Rebecca Louise does. Her four siblings tend to be more reserved.

At one point, Rebecca Louise became very angry, not only with her mother but with the whole world. She was tired of people asking about it, tired of the phone calls and tired of people being nosy. She just wanted to be left alone. But one thing remained very positive. She has developed a wonderful relationship with her brother and his family.

Rebecca Louise has felt lost. Her siblings have not lived through this journey like she has lived it. How fortunate they are that they don't get it, how fortunate they are for not having feelings of loneliness. She feels like she wouldn't put this on anyone and says "I'm glad it is me and not them". The one thing Rebecca Louise wants everyone to know is that "this journey never ends. For those who choose to start this journey, they need to know that this journey will never end. It will be there forever."

Chapter 10

———⌇———

TWO WEEKS BEFORE
CHRISTMAS, 2018

THE HOLIDAYS ARE so hectic. It was time for me to take a little break for searching for my biological family. Every holiday, birthday or special event I always imagined what my biological family would be doing. This particular Christmas was the same. I had been through so much in the past four years in my search. Joyce and I still kept in constant contact with each other. Joyce had become one of my biggest supporters and we had learned so many wonderful things about each other.

It is now exactly two weeks before Christmas, 2018. I had already put up the Christmas tree and decorated the house like I always do. I spent hours in the kitchen making cookies and sending them to William's office. It's just kind of my thing I love doing. And then the phone rings. It's Carol's phone number. Just like that I dropped everything and answered her call. Carol had just gotten an email from one of my third cousins. She had written this email six months earlier and had gotten no response. My third cousin, Kyle apologized for the delay in getting back to Carol. They had a new baby in their family. Kyle held the key to my search.

With the information Kyle provided, Carol was able to peg my biological mother. She told me who it was, where she lived, and that I have three sisters. Carol wasn't sure if my three sisters were half-sisters or full blood sisters. This was the best Christmas present EVER! I was thrilled.

But wait! I felt I had to have a heart to heart conversation with Carol. This is the third mother suspect. I had been disappointed two times during the last four years. I just didn't think I could handle another disappointment especially this time of year. How was Carol sure this was it? The information she had gotten from a third cousin after six months of waiting was exactly what she needed to put the puzzle of my life together. She assured me this was it. Once again, my faith kicked in. Okay, this is my mother, I have three sisters. Now what? First, to know my biological mother was alive was so amazing. Being sixty three and finding my biological mother was very rare. And what about my three sisters? Are we full blooded or half-sisters. To me it didn't make any difference. They're family!

We talked about making a connection. We even role played a phone call and different scenarios. I expressed my opinion about calling during the holidays. I just didn't want to disrupt anyone's Christmas holiday with this kind of life changing news. She assured me that I would know when the right time would be. I agreed.

Carol told me that my mother was an only child. Since I was born in the 1950's, having a child when you're a single woman was nothing like it is today. Many women were forced to relinquish their children for a better life. Often a family would make the decision to relinquish the child because of some dirty, little secret. And this dirty, little secret would be swept under the rug never to be discussed again. Later, I found out this to be somewhat true.

I told William of what Carol had found. William agreed that I should wait to make the first call. So here it is! It's Christmas and I now know who my biological mother is and that I have the names and phone numbers of my three sisters. But I did nothing. Absolutely, nothing.

I had been praying for the right time to make that first call. I knew

I wouldn't call my mother first because she is eighty two years old. Since I was most likely a dirty, little family secret, I chose not to call her. My empathy for her was overwhelming. I tried to imagine what she went through. My heart felt I should contact one of my sisters because we were all born one year apart. But I wasn't sure which one. How do I choose? I prayed God would tell me when the right time would be. Can you imagine what it was like to finally know you have biological family after looking for decades? You know who they are but the timing is all wrong to make contact. Yes, I wanted to immediately pick up the phone and make "that call". I've waited this long, a little bit more time won't hurt. This had become so gut wrenching.

Okay, it's time to breathe! At this time, I had been given a great gift. A gift of information, names of my biological family. It's Christmas and time to rejoice in the birth of our Lord and Savior, Jesus Christ.

Christmas came and went. All during the holiday I would wonder what my biological family was doing. Were they all opening presents together? Were they eating dinner together? My fantasy continued to go on and on. I had to make myself stop thinking about them and focus on my family, the family I love and the family that loves me.

I found myself looking at my sisters Facebook pages. They were all beautiful women. They looked happy and healthy. The resemblance was remarkable, especially Becky. In her wedding pictures we looked exactly alike. It looked like one of my sisters lived only four hours away from me. Wouldn't that be wonderful to take a trip to meet her since she lived so close? When I was looking at everyone's Facebook pages, I would try and figure out what my biological mother and father looked like. Were they married to each other? It was really hard to tell from the photos posted. I saw pictures of children, weddings, dinners, picnics and lots of wonderful times in their lives. I was in awe just looking at my sisters. I didn't really care if they were full blood or half-sisters. They're my family. To me, this was a major milestone after decades of wondering.

On New Year's Eve, my sister Ann called me. It wasn't unusual for

Ann to call me and wish me a Happy New Year! But when I answered the phone, I could hear overwhelming excitement when she said hello. My curiosity spiked. I asked her if she was okay and she said she was. She told me she had just gotten off the phone with a half-sister and they had agreed to meet. WOW. I was so happy for Ann. What a great way to start the new-year, meeting new family. I felt the Lord had revealed to me that it was time for me to "make that call."

During the rest of the evening and into the next morning, I rehearsed in my mind what I would say. There was so many different scenarios that could take place. I wanted to be prepared for any scenario that may play out. I had my list in my hand. I chose Gina. Gina is the youngest. I carefully dialed her number. My hand was shaking and my heart was pounding. In all my years of advertising, I had been trained how to make "cold calls" to prospective clients. I knew you had one shot to get it right on the first call. I knew I had to assure her I wasn't a scammer or a fake and that I was the real deal. I've never been shy but this call terrified me. I was ready for anything. The phone rang and no answer. I didn't leave a message. After all, what kind of message would you leave with the information I had? I hung up and checked the number to be sure I dialed correctly. It was the right number. Honestly, I felt deflated. I must keep my faith. God has opened this door for me, right now it was just a little stuck. I decided to sleep on this and regroup. Now, I'm glad I did.

The next morning, I dug a little deeper into Gina's Facebook page. Gina and her husband own a business. What if I call their business? Someone should answer the phone and at least let me know if Gina was in the office, right? Should I call her at work and talk about the kind of information I had? After all, this is life changing information. What have I got to lose? Will the door be a little stuck again?

I carefully dialed the phone number. A very nice male voice answered the phone. I asked if Gina was available. He said "no, she's not. Can I take a message for her?" Yikes, now what? I took a breath and said "yes, my name is Diane Gray" then gave him my phone number.

He asked what the call was in reference to. I said "it's a personal matter." One thing you need to remember in making a call like this is to make sure you are speaking directly to the right person. Never leave a message like "yes, I'm her long lost sister and I want to talk to her." He said OK. I could hear some hesitation in his voice. Little did I know that the male voice I was speaking to was Gina's husband?

About five minutes went by and my phone rang. It was Gina. I had programmed her phone number into my phone. Oh Lord, give me strength! This is it! This is the call that is about to change many lives. I had to be very careful and get it right. I answered the phone and the voice on the other end of the phone said "this is Gina. You had asked that I give you a call." I told her who I was. I explained that "I am an adoptee born at Ellis Hospital in Schenectady in July, 1955. I've been working with a genealogy researcher to find my biological family which has lead me to you." There, I said it. It's out there. I was direct and to the point. Gina continued to listen. I told her that she and her two sisters were my sisters. I wasn't sure if we were half-sisters or full blood sisters. There was dead silence on the other end of the phone. I asked her "are you still there?" She said yes. I explained that she must be in shock just like I am. She said she was. I really thought she'd hang up at this point but she didn't. To make sure she didn't think I was a scammer or a fraud, I told her where I grew up, the name of the school I went to, the name of the church I attended and some of my favorite places to go while I lived there. She said "this sure isn't the kind of call you get every day." I laughed and said I know what she means and that it wasn't the kind of call I made every day. After those comments, things got a little easier. She was in shock. Who wouldn't be? We talked for about thirty minutes. She told me that I had given her a lot of information and she wanted to do some research. I told her that she should. Gina said she'd get back to me. I told her she could call me if she had any questions and that she had my name and number. We hung up.

I never thought I would hear from Gina ever again. These calls are so difficult and stressful. I'm sure she tried to put herself in my shoes just as much as I was putting myself in her shoes. Any way you look at it, calls like this are very difficult. I kept going over the phone call over and over in my mind. Did I sound like a complete lunatic? Did Gina take me seriously? Would she tell her about the call? But more importantly, would Gina ever call me again? God will prevail!

I called Carol and told her I had talked to Gina. She was anxious to know how the call went. I told her what was said and that I tried to be reassuring to Gina that I was not a fraud or scammer. Carol said I did a good job. We both agreed that now we wait. It could happen later today, tomorrow, next month, or maybe never. I did a lot of pacing that day as I prayed. I stood firm and steadfast in my faith.

And just like that, Gina called me back the next day. I was shocked, happy, nervous, excited and as we say in the south, I was a hot mess. She said she had done some research. My heart was racing. She had called her sister Becky and told her what happened. They had scoured my Facebook page as well. They agreed how remarkable it was that we look so much alike. Gina told me Becky and her had called their dad and asked to meet him at the local coffee shop. They asked that he not bring his wife June when he came. They had something important to talk about. They assured him no one was sick or dead. He agreed to meet them. Gina told their dad of the conversation she and I had had the day before. He sat back in his chair, smiled and said "yes it's true." I was his daughter. Gina told me his shoulders came down as he smiled. He was relieved that "the cat was out of the bag."

They told him that I live in North Carolina. It seemed that he was so happy that not only the truth came out but that I was alright. Then he replied "when is she coming?"

I can only imagine how Gina and Becky must have felt knowing that their mother and father had a daughter that they didn't know about. They now knew the family secret, the secret of a daughter, their sister that was relinquished at birth. It all started a long time ago. Could these three sisters be understanding and have compassion not only for their parents and the decision they had to make decades ago, but can they accept the fact that they have an older sister?

This is more good news! I didn't have any information on my father at the time of my initial call with Gina. I had seen a picture of his head stone on findagrave.com. His birth date was on the stone but no date of death. I didn't think anything of that because it was almost two years after William's father died that we had his date of death engraved on his head stone. This is awesome news. My father is alive and he wants to meet me. I now have confirmation of three full blood sisters and a living father. God is good! We were all excited with the news. I told Gina I would make arrangements and get back with her. The phone call ended and a new beginning is happening.

But what about my biological mother? I knew she is still living and in the same area. Would she want to know about me? Would she want to meet me? In situations of re-connection you sometimes have to go with your best judgment. My best judgment was telling me not to pry and ask too many questions about my biological mother at this time. Let's just take baby steps.

William gets home and I'm a hot mess. I'm laughing and crying at the same time. I told him about the call. He too was excited. I think he was somewhat in shock just like I was. Who knew science and technology would get me to this point. DNA doesn't lie.

I told William I wanted to go and meet my family. I could take a flight and stay with Ann. Here's the problem. It was early January. It's bitter cold there and I'm not a fan of the cold. I said maybe I could go in March when it's a little warmer. William said no. I should go immediately. Your father is eighty two years old. I agreed. So I called Ann and told her the good news. I'm headed home to meet my three sisters and father. Maybe I'll be able to meet my biological mother too.

The next day I went into work and told them what days I would be off. I would be off eight days and that I would be meeting my biological family. I only work part time and when we ask for time off we usually get it. My request for the time off was denied. WHAT! My work family knew I had been looking for my biological family. They knew the whole story. Apparently, it was some kind of mandatory work weekend and I needed to be there because two other people were already off. WHAT! You can't tell me it's a mandatory work weekend and in the same breath say there's two people already off. That's just not fair. What part of mandatory do you not get? It's not like I've just decided to take a Caribbean vacation. I've found my biological family after searching for them for over fifty years. This is life changing experience for me. I ended up taking the following week off.

Ann and I were going to be busy. I was going to meet Ann's siblings and she would meet my siblings and father. This was going to be so much fun. It's not every day that two adopted sisters find their biological families at the same time. Furthermore, how often do two adopted sisters get to meet the others family together? It's mind blowing.

I had about a week to find winter clothing for my trip. Living in Eastern North Carolina retailers don't really carry lots of sweaters, boots, gloves and winter coats suitable for the super cold weather in upstate New York. On top of that it was after Christmas and spring clothes were adorning the shelves of retail establishments. I went to six stores to find the right kind of boots. It's really funny. While I was in on store trying on boots my sister Becky called during her lunch time. She asked what I was doing. I told her I had tried six different stores to try and find the right kind of boots that keep my feet warm. I told her I found hunting socks but boots were another story. I told her I just put on some nice boots that I really like. She said "size 10?" I said yes, how did you know? She said that's what size she wore. Oh my, we are sisters. Becky is the one sister that really looks like me. We got a big laugh out of that. We're starting to bond already.

So the big day has come. It was time for me to get on the plane and head north. It was beautiful in North Carolina. The sun was shining but it was just a little chilly. I had my big, new heavy coat over my arm. I knew I would need it when I got to Albany. Up north they were expecting snow. William took me to the airport and I checked in my luggage. The maximum weight for checking in luggage is forty pounds. Mine weighed thirty nine pounds. I am not used to wearing layers but it was mandatory where I was headed. First stop, Charlotte airport!

Getting to Charlotte was easy. Next stop, Albany, New York. I couldn't wait to see Ann. She was meeting me at the airport. On this leg of the trip there was about 130 people on-board. We were about twenty minutes from landing in Albany when the pilot came on over the intercom. He said we needed to stay seated and fasten our seat belts as the weather we were going to experience while landing in Albany was going to be bumpy due to the weather. I've been on some bumpy flights but this was the worst ever. The plane was shifting side to side and going up and down. None of the passengers said a word. You really could have heard a pin drop. I was clutching the armrests. I closed my eyes. I prayed to God to please place His hands on the steering wheel for the pilots and guide us all to safety. I've come this far and I sure didn't want to have something really bad happen. Have mercy on all souls on-board. It was a very bumpy landing during the snow storm. The pilot landed the plane and pulled up to the gate and shut down the engines. PHEW! That was the scariest twenty minutes I've ever had. Once the engines turned off, everyone on the plane stood up and applauded the pilots. There were praises of thanks for a well done landing. We all began to deplane and go our separate ways once we were inside the terminal.

I called Ann and she was down at the luggage carousels. I told her I'd be there in about five minutes. I was on the escalator and there she was. I struck a pose and said "She's back!" That meant I was back home. I was back at my roots after many, many years. There were lots of tears which turned to laughter while I told her about the bumpy landing. We grabbed my luggage and headed out to the snowy tundra. I think it was about ten degrees and it was dark and icy. We skated to the car, got in and I called William to tell him I made it in spite of the last twenty minutes of the flight.

I don't recall ever being so cold in my life. During my trip I don't think the temperature ever got over eleven degrees. It snowed, it rained and the ice was wicked. Ann got me settled in and we talked about the next day. By this time, Ann had met one of her half-sisters and her half-brother. She now had another half-sister that she had not met yet. We were going to meet them the next day for lunch. I was thrilled to be able to meet my sister's siblings. This was going to be the first day of an eight day journey that would forever change the lives of two sisters. So much had happened since those two weeks before Christmas. And now it's our time. God has blessed us by having the opportunity for meeting our biological family together.

Chapter 11

―――∽∾∽―――

MEETING ANN'S SIBLINGS

WHEN AN ADOPTEE is searching for lost family members, it's important to keep your family in the loop and have their support. My sister Ann's daughter Kristen is married and has grown children. Ann had explained to Kristen how important it was for her to find her biological family and get answers to her existence. Like most adoptees, Ann wanted to know who she looked like, who her biological parents were and if she had any siblings. Kristen didn't care at all and didn't understand what all the fuss was about.

I explained to Kristen that the next eight days were going to answer so many life-long questions for her mother and me. And if all went well, things were going to be magical and she would have a front row seat to watch it all unfold. I explained to Kristen that Ben and Adam, her cousins, were thrilled that I was in New York to get answers and meet my biological family. They were in full support of me coming to New York. Her mother needed her support too.

Our first day was to meet Ann's three siblings. Since Ann had met two of the siblings at an earlier get together, she was excited to meet another half-sister for the first time. It had snowed a little over night and the weather was bitter cold. I wore three shirts, heavy jeans, two pairs of socks, gloves, hat, scarf and boots and I was still freezing. We drove downtown to an authentic Italian restaurant. It's been fifty years since I had been to the town where I grew up. Ann drove past the church we used to attend. The snow was piled up high on each side of the streets we went down. Once we reached our destination, the snow was even piled up in the middle of the street. Parking was a mess but we managed. My sister warned me to just kind of "skate" across the ice. We held hands and "skated" that would make Dorothy Hamill proud. I was terrified. We landed on a cleaned off sidewalk that lead us to the restaurant.

It had been a long time since I had authentic Italian food. We told the hostess we were expecting three others as they lead us to a table. The aroma coming out of the kitchen was making my mouth water. We sat down and here comes Ann's siblings, Gayle, Don and Nancy. My first impression was that they all looked alike. They had the same eyes and nose. Nancy had curly hair just like Ann. They were all very kind and friendly. There were plenty of hugs, smiles and laughs and once again I had a front row seat to meeting my sister's siblings just like when I was with Rebecca Louise. God is so good!

Have you ever had Italian nachos? I highly recommend them. It's made from three kinds of sausage, smothered in cheese on top of homemade Italian chips. It's an appetizer we ordered to share but I could have made it a whole meal. The waiter and owner were wonderful. We had told them that we were all meeting new family. We actually stayed four hours.

During those four hours, we all got to know one another. Pictures of family, children and grand-children were shared. Gayle, Don and Nancy knew I had come up from North Carolina to meet my family. They were so excited to hear about how we found them. After giving the short version, they realized how God had really had his hand in everything we had done. I told Don that we were meeting my three sisters tomorrow for lunch first then going to meet my father later in the week. I admitted I was a little nervous and that you just never know how things will turn out. I fell in love with my sisters siblings. In fact, I told Don that if it didn't work out with meeting my family I wanted to pile on with their family. Don looked at me, smiled and said "you're already in!" I got very teary eyed. Those words were very kind and I will never forget them. Jokingly, I said I'd get back with him on that. They even wanted my phone number so I could text them and let them know how it went. I kept thinking that Kristen doesn't know what she's missing. These people that I just met are so amazing and they're family! They are her aunts and uncle. I prayed Kristen would change her mind and come with Ann and I to meet my sisters the next day.

We had been in the restaurant for quite some time. They were transitioning from lunch to setting up for dinner. The owner came over to our table and told us to stay as long as we wanted. He knew what was going on. Once again, my faith in mankind was restored. Honestly, I can't tell you what I had for lunch, except for the nachos but I will tell you I will never forget that day.

Later that night, Ann, her husband Will and I talked about our four hour lunch. I'm so glad Will is in Ann's life. He's very supportive of this entire new chapter in her life.

Chapter 12

———∽∾———

MY THREE SISTERS

THINGS WERE BECOMING surreal. My big day was finally here. I was going to meet my three full blood sisters for lunch. Ann and I invited Kristen to come with us and we were thrilled when she said she'd meet us for lunch. I believe Kristen was beginning to realize how important meeting new family really is. She knows I wouldn't leave William for eight days, travel over 850 miles in January on a very turbulent plane ride, in a huge snow storm, with temperature never getting over eleven degrees if this wasn't really seriously about to change her mother's life as well as mine. Let's not forget relentless shopping for winter clothes in North Carolina in January when stores were selling tee shirts, flip flops, bikinis and shorts. Kristen is a very smart woman, I knew she'd change her mind.

Kristen met us at the restaurant for lunch. I told her I was so glad she came and how much it meant to me. I told her the story of my friend Rebecca Louise and how I was with her the day she found her brother after twenty nine years. And how the day before I was front row center with her mother meeting her siblings. It can be very emotional and brought my heart so much joy. Magic was about to happen and now she was going to be front row center to see complete strangers meet for the first time that are family.

Moments later Joyce walked in. I left my seat at the table and walked towards her with tears in my eyes. We were both crying and laughing at the same time. What a joyous moment! We both had red hair and look so much alike. We commented on each other's hair color and laughed because both of us had color right out of a bottle. My first impression of Joyce is that she is filled with love. She's a lover of the Lord, beautiful inside and out. Next thing I knew Becky comes through the door. Oh my Lord! We do look alike. No introductions were needed. More tears were flowing. I told her I felt like I was looking in the mirror. Becky is also very beautiful, has kind eyes and a killer smile. WOW! She said Gina was parking the car.

Next thing I know Gina comes through the door. My youngest sister also looks like me. I've hit the sister jack pot! She too is very sweet, beautiful, extremely intelligent and very kind. We also hugged. I didn't think I ever stopped crying. All three of my sisters are wonderful women.

I was so thankful for this very moment in time. My dream of finding and meeting my biological family was coming true. Decades of wondering and searching were now here in this restaurant with my adoptive family and my biological family. God is good!

As we sat at the table, I was looking at each one of them and giving Him thanks. We talked about our families, our children and grandchildren. It was almost like we knew each other but had not seen each other in a while. I know that may sound a little weird but that's exactly how I felt. My sisters were so easy to talk to and get to know. We even remarked how our hands were alike.

We also talked about how I had actually found them. Explaining that being adopted from New York State, having an original birth certificate was out of the question. They were all sealed. I explained that I had taken two DNA tests and sent a request for my non-identifying information from the state's Health Department. I also told them about how Carol, my search angel was able to take my DNA matches and non-identifying information to narrow the search. I even told them that I had two suspects as possible biological mothers that did not work out. And then I told them about how my third cousin match supplied Carol with the missing piece of the puzzle that lead me to them (my three sisters) and biological mother. After four and a half years of Carol's hard work, here I am, sitting in this restaurant with my three full blood sisters. Each of them were in awe of how it all happened.

We all took turns telling a little bit about ourselves. How does one tell their life story of over sixty years in an "elevator speech"? Of course, there would be more time to take a further glimpse in all of our lives. One thing that struck me was how Joyce and I paralleled in many aspects of our lives. She has lived in quite a few places and so have I. We laughed and called ourselves gypsy soul sisters. As it turns out, we really are. One thing for sure, our common thread is the DNA that runs through our veins. We are sisters.

Gina told me that she didn't think that their mother would be willing to meet me. Although I tried to hide my disappointment, I said that was OK and that I fully understand how she may feel. It's not every day that you're sixty something daughter that you relinquished at birth pops up out of nowhere. Little did I know I would learn more about the circumstances of my birth and adoption later in the week?

I was so thrilled to have Ann and Kristen with me that monumental day. I couldn't have done it without them. Yes, there were tears but there was a lot of laughter too. I knew my biological parents must have had a sense of humor because their daughters sure do.

I'm sure everyone around us was wondering what was happening with six women who were laughing like crazy one minute then crying the next. Our waitress asked if it was a family reunion. I spoke up and told her I was adopted and was meeting my three beautiful sisters for the first time and that I had my sister and niece with me as well. She got choked up too and told us she was trying to find her biological brother. Even the owner of the restaurant told us to stay as long as we liked. It's not every day that a group of sisters get together for the first time in that particular restaurant. It just proved once again how good people actually are.

The afternoon just seemed to fly by. We had spent almost four hours together. We talked about getting together on Thursday at my biological fathers home. He and June would have lunch ready for us all. Ann and I found out what his favorite cookies and ice cream were and told them we would bring them with us on Thursday.

The time came where everyone had to get home to their families. I didn't want the day to end. It warmed my heart to know and see for myself just how accepting of me they really are. They're so much like me, they have room in their hearts to love a new family member.

That night back at Ann's house we talked about how the day went. I told her I was so happy how it went and how I couldn't wait to meet my biological father. We both remarked how we all looked alike and what exceptional women my sisters truly are. I told Ann that both of us had hit the sibling jack pot.

We decided that the next day, Wednesday would be our day together, just the two of us to do whatever we wanted to do. We decided to take a little day trip.

Our Wednesday morning started out with coffee and lots of conversation. Our plan was to drive a little further upstate. Ann wanted to go by and see the home our parents owned before they moved to Virginia to retire. Our first stop was at a consignment store that is owned by a friend of Ann's. As usual, our shopping trips included looking everything over about five times. Our shopping is quite an undertaking. "Hey check this out", "you need this", "try this on, it's your color". I just love my sister. We finally checked out and loaded up the car. I realized there was no way I could get this stuff home. It was decided we'd keep shopping and ship my valuable new purchases home.

Our next stop was just a few miles down the road to see mom and dad's old house. Their home was located slightly out of the township limits heading down a beautiful country road. The town is very quaint with gingerbread style homes and well-manicured yards. Main Street was lined with maple trees. I remember the maple leaves turning beautiful shades of red, orange and yellow during the fall. You could almost smell the pine trees while driving past the hillside. We were both pleased to see their old homestead was kept up by the new owners. It appeared to have a fresh coat of paint. They still had a few acres of magnificent blue spruce trees. The neighbor's barn was still there too. It too was in magnificent shape. There had been many great memories made right where I was standing, memories Ben and Adam still talk about when we came up from Virginia to see them. Oh how I wish I could take my grandchildren on a sleigh ride down some of these hills.

Next stop, back to the old neighborhood where we really grew up. The trip took about an hour. I don't think we stopped talking the entire day. We were doing some serious reminiscing. As we pulled into the old neighborhood, I couldn't believe how clean and tidy all the houses are. It had been fifty years since I've traveled down these roads in our neighborhood. Most of these houses looked like they had some serious make-overs. I remember walking to "the square" to catch the bus to school. "The square" was actually just that. It is a big square in the middle of the neighborhood. It had just the right incline to sleigh ride in the winter. During the summer we would skateboard there and just "hang out" with friends. Our parents actually owned three different houses in the same neighborhood. This was the neighborhood I grew up in, it was the neighborhood I walked to school in, it was the neighborhood where all my friends and I grew up in. These neighbors and friends were the ones I truly missed when we moved to Virginia in 1969.

That night, Ann made the cookies to take the next day. We would pick up the ice cream on the way to my father's house.

Chapter 13

———~~———

TODAY I MEET DAD

IT IS THURSDAY, the day I was to meet my biological father. Please feel free to grab a box of tissues now. You're gonna need them!

It had snowed again, of course. The sky was gray and it was bitter cold outside. The thermometer read eleven degrees. I'm so glad I brought a lot of clothes for layering. The car was sitting on a huge ice patch. I'm thinking there's no way to even get to the car let alone get it off the ice patch. Here comes Will to the rescue. He moved the car and escorted us safely into the car. He's such an amazing person! I felt like a really old lady being escorted out to the car by a young whipper snapper. We speculated the drive would take about an hour and a half because of the crazy road conditions. Nothing was going to stop us today!

It was a beautiful drive. The mountains were beautiful. The ice covered rivers seemed to wind around giving us glimpses of sparkle from the snow. We finally arrived and pulled in the driveway. Becky met us outside and told us to come through the kitchen because it would be easier. That was fine with me. The last thing I needed was to take a tumble on the ice at this very important time in my life and wind up in the hospital with a broken bone!

I remember grabbing Ann's hand as I paused just before going inside. I looked at her with tears in my eyes and said "this is it. This is what I've been waiting for." She gave me a huge smile. She didn't need to say a word. She knew!

The door opened and we went in. There were lots of people. I recognized my sisters, that's all I knew. Suddenly, it happened…right there in my father's kitchen. He entered from the other side of the kitchen. Magically, people parted. Things seemed to be surreal, moving in slow motion. But just like that, we walked towards each other. I never have felt such a powerful and emotional hug in all my years. It was meant to be. My dad was hugging me. Both of us were sobbing. I am here! This is my moment. God sent me here. There wasn't a dry eye in the house.

My father looked at me and said "I didn't ever want to let you go, I think about you every day and I love you". I will never forget these words. He told me how beautiful I was. I told him he needed to get his eyes examined. That got everyone laughing. He knew I had been looking for a long time and thanked me for my perseverance. I explained to him how my faith kept me going over the years and that God would make this all possible in His time. I told him that at the time I had made contact with Gina, I didn't know he was living. I told him I found a picture on Ancestry of his headstone. I showed him a picture of the headstone and commented that there was no date of death. I said, "Now I know why. You aren't dead yet." Thank God! That started more laughter.

I introduced him to my sister Ann and told him that earlier in the week we had met some of her siblings. He just couldn't believe how wonderful the whole story was. I told him I had a little gift for him. I had put together a little photo album. I told him that by giving me up for adoption that he had done something truly amazing for me. He had given me an opportunity to have a new life and that had been wonderful. In fact, I told him just how wonderful and pulled out the photo album. I explained that by giving me up for adoption it had changed the lives of many people he would never know. I had pictures of when I was little and growing up. I showed him pictures of my mom and dad and my childhood. I told him he has two grandchildren and showed him the pictures. Then I got to the pictures of my grandchildren, his great grandchildren. I had current pictures of my two granddaughters and my grandson. He was thrilled and wanted to know when he could meet them. He asked me about my grandson. I said "he likes to go fishing. Do you like to go fishing?" He replied he didn't. I told him that that was okay because he'd love to ride on some of those fancy tractors of his. I don't remember seeing my father not smile during the entire day.

My father told me how different things were when I was born. He told me he wasn't given the opportunity to have a say so in my adoption. He wanted to keep me. It was difficult on him. His parents, my paternal grandparents, were upset about my adoption as they were never given the opportunity to establish a relationship with me. My biological mother and father married four months after I was born. I knew it was important for me not to just blurt out questions I had always had surrounding my adoption. I knew in time I would learn more. For now, let's just get to know one another.

I met my sister's husbands. I met my fathers wife June. She had made lunch for all of us. June is a very kind woman. It felt like everyone was truly amazed how this whole situation happened. I was the sister they didn't know about. I am the oldest sister, the family secret. And here I was.

The next thing I knew, someone was at the door. In walked a very attractive woman and man. I was introduced to them. It was my biological father's sister and her husband, Sue and Gary. One of the first things I noticed right away were Sue's boots. They were bright red. Heart be still, I'm in love with this woman. Her earrings were also red. She has such a warm smile and sparkle in her eyes. She definitely was my father's sister, my aunt. Gary has a sense of humor that kept us all laughing.

We all wandered into the living room. Sue asked me to sit next to her which I gladly did. She told me that the rocking chair I was sitting in had been in the family for many years. We talked about how wonderful it was that this day had happened. At one point she put her hand on my arm, looked me in the eye and said "you're good people, you're a keeper". My eyes began to water once again. I told her I loved her boots. We all got a good laugh.

I remember looking around the room in amazement. This is the day I had been waiting for. This is my biological family. A few weeks ago we were total strangers. Now we are family, family that has not only accepted me but have also accepted Ann. Not only that, but I look like them. They're good people. I wished William was here to see this. God has blessed me.

My father told me that he works every day. He is 83 years old. He said that if he didn't get up and go to work every day then that would be the day that he died. I found out that my father is extremely healthy and longevity is prominent in the family. That is really good to know. There are no health issues with cancer, major organ issues, just a strong and healthy lineage.

My father kept going through the photo album I gave him. He would pause at the pictures of my grandchildren and smile. He knew this was a blessing. We talked about my parents for a while. I told him my mother was a registered nurse but once Ann and I came along she became a stay at home mom. My father worked as a nuclear engineer for the Navy. I told him I had been given every opportunity available to me and that I was happy and healthy. He mentioned again that he wished my biological mother would agree to see me. I told him that it was OK and maybe one day soon she would change her mind. I just wanted to tell her thank you for giving me the gift of life. I wanted her to know she did the right thing giving me away and that I did not want to have her go to her grave feeling overwhelmed with grief and shame because of the circumstances 64 years ago. I pray that one day we can at least talk on the phone.

My father asked me what kind of work I had done. I told him I was retired but work part time in the bridal industry and that I had owned my own bridal boutique for eight years. And before that I had spent a majority of my career in radio sales. He was so thrilled that I was so happy. His smile never left his face the entire day. After all, I am his daughter, his daughter that he had never seen. The sheer magnitude of the day would be remembered for all of us forever.

It was time for Ann and I to start our journey back to her house. We were all going to Gina's house in two days for brunch. I knew this would be such a fun time too. My sister has invited all of us to her home. This is a great way to spend the day with family before I had to head back to North Carolina.

All during the drive back to Ann's house we talked about not only how wonderful the day had been but the whole trip of meeting each other's family. We wondered what our parents would be thinking about it. Both of us agreed they probably would approve. I told Ann that I couldn't have gotten through this journey without her beside me holding my hand.

Back at Ann's house I became a little antsy. I was pacing the floor wringing my hands together. Ann asked if I was OK. I told her I was fine and that I was feeling the power of the Lord's presence. I was feeling so very blessed for the people in my life. The Lord was telling me that my faith had been strong and my perseverance had been my blessing. The power and message was very strong to me. Ann and I talked about how blessed we both have been.

Later that night, lying in bed I pulled out my phone and looked at the pictures I had taken. I looked at the pictures of my sisters and was feeling very thankful. Then I looked at pictures of me and my father, my eyes filled with tears. This day was the day I'd dreamed of. I looked out the window. It was a clear night sky with stars shining bright. I knew my dad was looking at the same stars too. We now had found what we had been looking for—each other. "Good night dad. I love you" I said. I slept more soundly than I had in years.

Chapter 14

A FAMILY DINNER

THE NEXT DAY Ann and I spent some time in the kitchen. We were having family over for dinner. We told them we had something to tell them. It was going to be exciting to have them over for dinner and tell them our story. Ann warned me that some reactions would be rather cold and would not think what had happened would be a big deal. Some people are just like that especially if they don't understand what adoptees go through in their lives. Regardless of their reactions, our journey of the past few days would be told.

One by one family came to the house. It was still bitter cold and had snowed even more. Being from North Carolina, I don't think I ever truly got warm while I was there. But the warmth in my heart kept me going. This was a trip of a lifetime that two sisters experienced together.

Ann is a fabulous chef. Everything she makes turns out delicious. She had made lots of chili. Some family members I had not seen in years came. Kids had grown taller, older kids were telling about their new career, and some were telling me about school. It was so much fun to sit, laugh and eat. Of course everyone kept asking what was going on. It wasn't every day that Ann's sister came to New York and especially in the worst snow storm of the season. Ann and I would look at each other and grin. We told them no one was sick or dying and that we'd tell them after dinner. Some family members tried so hard to figure out what was going on. We would not say a word!

After dinner we gathered in the living room. Ann wanted me to tell the story. I laughed and told her that according to my DNA I am not prone to be afraid of public speaking. I thought that since it was her house, she'd tell the story. But no, it was up to me.

I started out by telling them that I was so happy to be here with them, in spite of the cold weather. But I had to come. I reminded them that Ann and I were both adopted. We had always wondered who our biological family is. Are our biological parents alive, do we have brothers and sisters out there? I explained that over four years ago I had taken a DNA test "to see what's out there." When I got the results I explained that I learned I was English, Irish and Welch, not Dutch like I had grown up thinking I was. I even had biological matches but couldn't understand what I was really looking at. I also explained that I joined several Facebook pages that helped adoptees find biological family. My comment on Facebook was "I've taken a DNA test and gotten my results. I don't understand them. Now what?" Much to my surprise a woman named Carol offered to help me. She is a search angel. Carol guided me through the process and made suggestions of other types of information available to me. After taking yet another DNA test and supplying Carol with additional information, she was able to trace back to my very beginning. That beginning was just a few counties over. During the four long, emotional years I would talk to Ann. She became curious about her adoption as well. She too did a DNA test and Carol was willing to help her as well.

I explained to them how we both found our families at about the same time which was two weeks before this past Christmas. And this is what brings me here now. Ann and I met several of her siblings and I have met my father and three full blood sisters. I also explained that it was rare for two adoptees to find family at our age, especially at the same time. At that point I wrapped it up. Sometimes too much information is an overload. Some were thrilled and some seemed rather nonchalant about it. And that's okay. We told them. Maybe they thought one of us had won the lottery and were going to share it with them. Who knows? But in my book, we did win the lottery and in a big way.

I pulled Ann aside and told her she was right…some really could have cared less. I asked her if I told the story right. Was I long winded? She said I did it right. I whispered in her ear "tough crowd". We got a good laugh out of it. One thing's for sure, we all had a great time and it was wonderful to see them. After all, it's family!

On our next visit, we were invited to Gina's home for brunch. It had snowed again. Kristen, Will, Ann and I braved the snow for a long drive. Will thought it would be fun to take the back roads. As we were riding along, he would point out places he had been. I made a remark of how blue the ice was on sides of rocky hills. He told me that the ice was really thick there and it would be a long time for the ice to completely melt in the spring. The bluer the ice, the thicker it was. We finally reached our destination. It was wonderful to have everyone together. My father was so pleased for all of us to be under one roof at the same time. I would look over at him when he wasn't looking and saw him grinning with delight. He kept remarking how happy he was that I had persevered to find them. June told me how happy he was. I remember pulling Ann aside and whispering to her "this is my family." Tears of joy were flowing. I felt like God had really favored not only me but my family as well. I wished William could have been there. My dream of having a big family was happening at that very moment. The only thing different is that they were real faces unlike my dream where faces were blurred. They were real voices, there was real laughter and there was real joy.

I found it truly interesting that Will actually knew Becky's husband. What a wonderful coincidence! The next thing I knew I was presented with a balloon that said "It's a girl" on it. Dad had me sit on his lap with the balloon. It was a great laugh! The next thing I knew, a birthday cake was presented to Gina. What a great way to celebrate.

The time seemed to fly by. It was time to get back to Ann's house. In my heart I knew this would be the last time I would see everyone on this trip. Saying goodbye that day was not easy but I knew my trip would end and I would be heading back home in less than two days.

The next day Ann and I met our cousin and his wife for lunch. It had been too many years since we had seen each other. In fact, it was at my mother's funeral when we were all together. I told Ann it was her turn to tell them what was going on. My feeling after Ann told them is that they really did get it. My cousin really grasped the whole trip and its meaning and thought it was amazing. I remember he stopped, leaned back in his chair and said "wow". I remember saying "yup, it's a BIG WOW". We also told him how extremely rare it was for two adopted sisters to find their biological families at the same time. He has a sister who is also adopted and he wondered if she ever thought about finding her biological family. Ann had said they had exchanged a few emails about that very subject but knew it was fear that was holding her back. This was the last of our family that we would see on this trip. I was going home the next day.

The next morning was really tough. Ann drove me to the airport. I told her not to park in the parking deck, just drop me off at the curb. We sat there for a few minutes. We both talked about this amazing eight days we spent together. She told me I need to write a book. I just kind of laughed it off. It was very difficult for me to get out of the car. A huge part of me wanted to stay and spend more time with new family and my always family. I couldn't pull away. My heart was torn. More and more tears were flowing. Then I looked at Ann and said "William needs me. We're so happy together and he is my heart." Sometimes just sitting there in silence holding someone's hand is the right thing to do. I told Ann I loved her and got out of the car and faded into the crowd.

When I arrived at my final destination, seeing William standing there waiting for me was the best thing ever. I was happy to be in his arms again. I told him it was the best trip he could have ever given me, the gift of family! It really was a trip of a lifetime for me. I told him it would probably take time for me to tell him about it since there was so much to tell. After all, we have a lifetime together.

Chapter 15

ANN'S STORY

How do you start writing a chapter for a book about being adopted when you realize upon reflection that your whole emotional life has been impacted and you're 69 years old? That's my dilemma as I put pen to paper. There have been so many experiences in my life that were shaped. Sometimes subtlety by the fact that I was adopted. Had I been raised in a more traditional family without any question as to my own identity I may have made different choices and my journey might have been so different. I'm not saying that my life has been bad, on the contrary. It just might have been different. Because growing up knowing you were adopted raises so many questions about who you are, but most especially, in my case at least, the biggest question I had was why I wasn't good enough to keep? My biggest worry as a child was that my mom and dad would decide to give me back. They would find out what my biological mother already knew; I was not a keeper. Make no mistake. I loved the parents who raised me, but as a child, despite being told I was loved, there was always that nagging fear. Mom and dad never knew that was how I felt. I couldn't risk telling them. I knew I was not a keeper and didn't measure up to other kids, but if they hadn't figured it out, I wasn't going to tell them. It was a child's reasoning of course. Even as I grew older and better understood those childish notions persisted, and I didn't even realize it.

I understand that all people have things happen in their lives that are difficult. I'm by no means unique in any way. And I wouldn't even call being an adoptee difficult. However, I'm guessing that many other adoptees probably had similar insecurities to mine. Had my parents known how I felt, I'm sure they would have reassured me, but I probably wouldn't have believed them. And I definitely wouldn't have believed them when my sister came along. But I'm getting ahead of myself.

Let's start at the beginning. When I was very young my mother read a book to me about Little Bob & Mary whose parents chose them. She explained that I was different and had been chosen too. To me, that meant that my other mother didn't want to keep me and that if mom and dad chose me, they could also choose to give me back. I don't know how old I was when the realization hit, but no matter. The die was cast!

For me, the beginning is my first memory. I was lying on my back in a dark room. Although it was dark, there was enough light to see. It was ambient light coming through several windows on a long wall. The room was very large and there were many beds just like the one I was in. I assume they also had occupants but that wasn't my focus. I was watching a woman across the room in a chair. I was very afraid, cold and crying. Although the woman was watching me too, she made no effort to come to me. I badly wanted her to. Fade out! I carried that memory/dream often when I was young.

The next memory was of me sitting in a sandbox with another child in our back yard. My mother and another woman were sitting some distance away, or so it seemed, on lawn chairs. The other child started crying and both women ran down to us. I didn't understand what was happening but I was scared. I saw something red running down the child's arm. My mother and the other woman's face were knotted up as they scooped the child up and ran to the house, leaving me in the sandbox. I thought I had done something horribly wrong and I would be left in the sandbox forever. Fade out on that memory! As an adult I asked my mother about the incident. My mother was shocked that I remembered it and that I had described it accurately. As she explained it, there had been a piece of broken glass in the sandbox. The little boy had cut himself. The other woman and my mother panicked and ran him up to the house to wash and bandage the wound. My mother was a nurse. Of course after this injury was addressed, mom remembered she had left me down at the sandbox and ran down to get me. I hadn't remembered that part. What stuck with me was that maybe I had done something terrible to that child and my mother left me because of it. I was only a year and a half old. Who knows? It seems so strange to me that a child that young would think that way. When and why did I start feeling that something about me was defective?

Both of these memories are overwhelming experiences of panic and fear. I had several other early memories. One was of my mother opening the front door and me holding on to her for dear life as our giant horse of a boxer came galloping in and knocked me down as always, licking my face all over. While that was fear, it was different. It was more excitement, like being on a carnival ride, the anticipation of an extreme sensation. That describes the level of fear experienced by most kids, I think. I'm not so sure the fear of abandonment is felt by all children, adopted or not but it was certainly a keen emotion for me. I'm guessing it might be a universal experience of adoptees.

Early memories were not all doom and gloom. I remember holding my dad's hand on my second birthday as he opened our front door and our neighbor handed me a book with a yellow ribbon wrapped around it. The cover was a picture of a beautiful girl in a yellow gown standing by a giant pumpkin. All around the outside of the book the pages were gilded in gold. It was the most beautiful thing I had ever seen, and it was for me! My dad took me upstairs and tucked me into bed and read me the book. As each page turned, I was overcome by the beautiful illustrations. The book was Cinderella, and I felt as though I was there in those pages. I believe that was the beginning of my love of art which has remained a constant throughout my life. So as you see, not all of my memories were bad. It's just that the bad memories had a common theme of abandonment and not being good enough.

My mother made a special effort to assure my sister and me that we were chosen. For me, that meant brought up the question why we were available to be chosen. I don't know how old I was when I understood that most families didn't happen like ours but I must have been quite young. That brings me to the tragedy of my sister.

The pain I felt when you arrived was certainly magnified a thousand fold because of being adopted. I was such a sensitive child. Mom always referred to me as deep. And so the worst day of my life happened when I was almost five.

The beginning of that day started like any other. As I remember it, mom, dad and I took a drive. I'm not sure now if it was a taxi or our own car. I remember my mother talking to me and she was happy. We parked and went inside a building where we were greeted by a woman who told me to wait as she ushered my parents into another room and closed the door. I was afraid because it seemed so unfamiliar and strange. Despite the fear I remained quietly stoic since mom had said it was okay. When the door opened and my parents came back into the room I realized that things were about as far from okay as it was possible to get. My mother was carrying a baby! My worst fear had been realized. They did know I was defective and they got another one to replace me! I was devastated! Mom didn't even look at me during the car ride home. Of course I understand now that they couldn't warn me as they didn't know when a baby would be available for them. The baby was a surprise to them as it was for me. Just like that, it was all over for me. It was classic sibling rivalry with the added twist of me waiting to be sent packing because my sister was better in every way. She was an extrovert and a ham even as a baby. I was shy. She demanded and got all the attention. Of course being a baby she needed more attention. My parents would fuss over her and laugh until I wanted to wretch!

To make things even worse, we moved to California that year. My parents went by themselves to find and buy a house, leaving my sister with our aunt and me with my grandmother. I had met my grandmother many times but I had never stayed at her house. I'm sure my parents told me otherwise but I was convinced that they had given me to her and kept my sister. The ax had fallen! Here it was. I would be living with a scary old woman whose house smelled funny and there were no kids around to play with. I was only with her for three weeks and she was perfectly nice but three weeks is a long time for a scared little kid whose hoping her parents come back for her. My grandmother worked at a very prominent college as a librarian. While she was at work she left me at daycare. I was uncooperative and cried all day. The alternative plan was that I sit in a corner of the library all day across from the circulation desk staring at Gram. I remember it all so clearly. One day I lucked out! A student asked about me and offered to take me across the street for ice cream. She felt sorry for me. Gram said yes and she walked toward me holding out her hand. She was the most beautiful girl I had ever seen. She looked just like Cinderella. The point is she recognized a terrified child and was kind enough to take me every day for ice cream and to her apartment until Gram was ready to take me home. She made me feel safe for a while and I am grateful to this day. Later, Gram had told my mother about the beautiful student who had taken me to her apartment for ice cream. When I was in my teens, my mother thought I was old enough to know who the beautiful Cinderella was. Cinderella was the famous movie star Jane Fonda.

Finally, the long weeks were over and my parents came for me. You'd think that their return would have dispelled my fears but it didn't. The self-doubt has become a part of who I am today.

As my sister grew I became acutely aware of the fact that I was different, the odd one out. Among many other things my sister shared my parent's sense of humor. I did not. My mother often pointed out I had no sense of humor. In fact, I certainly did but just found different things funny. My sister was my dad's favorite but she was a thorn in my side. Even though she was adopted, she fit in. I did not. Mom would tease me about being odd. I am sure it was meant to be innocent but I felt hurt and not good enough. Again, I am not a keeper. How much of this emotional baggage was attributed to my being adopted? A lot I think. My poor sister. It wasn't her fault.

My teen years were tumultuous. I kept so much pain and insecurity hidden. I felt both parents were disgusted with me, I had let them down. It's not that I wanted to. I was flawed and they knew they'd been stuck with a dud. My dad and I had issues. He could be uncommunicative and harsh with me. In all fairness, I was a sulky child sometimes and very insecure. Obviously mom and I got along sometimes. At other times we did not. There were so many times during those years that I wondered who my real family was. Who was I? If I was so unlike my adoptive family, was there anyone in the world that I was like? It was not possible to discuss my adoption with mom. The few times I tried to talk to her about it she would get very upset and cried proclaiming herself to be my only mother. Of course I understand this now how she felt. I understood then, too. But it meant so much to me to know who I was. Where did I come from? Why had I been given up? I never wanted to hurt her. I loved her. My father didn't talk about it. It was totally out of the question.

There was never much communication of any sort going on in our house. I grew up feeling very alone. This wasn't my parents fault. It was indicative of the times and certainly reflected how they had been raised. I'm sure teenage angst was also to blame. When a person feels they're not good enough to be loved they end up searching for it. At least I did.

I always wanted to have a boyfriend and I did have several. Feeling loved was of paramount importance to me. I chased them away with my neediness, then on to the next. It was all that mattered to me in life at that age. I was a mildly rebellious teen. Combine that with the cultural explosion of the late 1960's you can imagine the fireworks in my home and life. I ended up quitting college, getting a job and moving out when I was 18. My parents and sister moved several states away and we were estranged for a while. How I wish I had been able to talk to them honestly back then. I don't know if knowing my biological parents would have made a difference in my attitudes about myself or my adoptive parents growing up but it would have changed things in some ways for sure. At the very least it would have encouraged dialogue and I'd like to believe that knowing the circumstances of my biological mother would have enabled me to feel compassion for her and facilitated the understanding that I had value and it wasn't about me.

I've focused the story so far on my youth. This is when the stigma of adoption really impacts us, our formative years. Life moved forward. I married, became a mom myself and went through many dramas and life events as we all do. Widowhood, remarriage, another child, grandchildren, divorce and fires. Some of it hard but I see most of my life as joyful and good. I've been so blessed by God and I'm grateful every day. I've had a wonderful life. Often I find myself looking around corners and into so many faces wondering if there was a connection. That question never goes away, never. You tell yourself it doesn't but the question is always there. There's always a weight on your shoulders you've always endured but didn't know you carried until you find the truth. When that happens, the weight floats away and you finally feel free. For the first time, you know who you are and you are free.

I've shared this back story so you, the reader could perhaps understand what a profound experience it has been to finally find my family this late in the game. I would have never have thought it possible! Last year my wonderful sister urged me to submit a sample of my DNA to Ancestry.com. She had tried another site first and had been searching for her family for three years. A search angel named Carol had contacted her and told her what steps to take. New York State has been a difficult state as all adoption records were sealed. That has recently changed and what a blessing this is for so many people. Carol is

experienced in reading genealogical information and searching generations of public records. My sister encouraged me to contact her as well,
so I did. After the DNA results were posted, I was contacted by one of
my matches who believed I was his cousin or his aunt. When respond-
ing to him I told him my age. He wrote back and said I was his aunt.
Then a miracle happened. He sent me photographs of my biological
mother! He also sent photographs of his dad and his baby picture. I
cried. To be seeing my mother's beautiful face for the first time felt
like a miracle! Carol called me and confirmed my mother's identity.
Unfortunately, she died young. But I finally knew! She was 17 when I
was born. It must have been terribly difficult for her. I will be grateful
to her for the rest of my life for having me. I wish I could have met her
and known her. Coincidentally, Will and my biological mother share
the same birthday! I have a half-brother who I haven't met but we have
been in touch. I also have a half-sister. We have also communicated but
never met. I understand I may have been quite a surprise and they may
not want to meet. I understand and respect their privacy. However, I
do hope that someday we can meet.

Once again Carol called to tell me she had found my father. I had
also been contacted by a cousin who said they believed they knew
who my father was. They were sending his mother's DNA sample to
Ancestry.com and if his mother tested out as my aunt, he would contact my father's daughter and let her know she had a sister. The test
results turned out she was my half-sister! My half-sister called me on
New Year's Eve. It was shortly after we met along with one of my brothers. Soon after that I met another half-sister and three more brothers along with nieces and nephews. They are wonderful people and
I feel I am home when I am around them. The more I get to know
them, the more traits I see in common. I now know my nationality!
Unfortunately, my biological family is deceased. But I do have this big
and beautiful family whom I already love. My life is changed forever.
Thank you God!

In retrospect, for the most part I have let go of all those old insecurities a long time ago. I'm older now and let's hope wiser. I realize these insecurities serve no purpose. All of us are different or may seem odd in one way or another. Who really cares anyway? Knowing who I am and where I came from has brought me joy and peace.

Coincidentally, when I had told my sister about the call I had received on New Year's Eve from my half-sister, it was at that moment she had decided to finally reach out to her family for the first time. Carol had told her about two weeks before Christmas about her biological family. She was waiting for the right time to reach out to her biological family. She now knew it was her time to make that call. Who would ever imagine that two sisters who were adopted would ever find their own biological families at the same time? God sure does know what he's doing!

It was several weeks later when my sister came up from North Carolina and we spent eight days together meeting each other's biological family. This is just the beginning of our journey. What a wonder filled life! The truth will set you free

Chapter 16

Children's Home Society of North Carolina

As I was developing the concept of this book and gathering information and research, I found an ad on Facebook talking about an upcoming informational meeting for fostering to adoption. At this informational seminar, attendees would learn about Children's Home Society, fostering and adoption of children. William and I were not interested in fostering or adoption as we were preparing for retirement but I was interested in adoption. Being an adoptee from New York, I thought it would be interesting to know what was happening in North Carolina.

I contacted to seminar leader, Darius Moore and explained to him that I had seen the Facebook ad about the upcoming seminar. I further explained that I wasn't particularly interested in fostering or adopting but that I was writing a book about adoption. He was on board with the idea.

The day of the seminar was truly wonderful. Darius talked about CHS, how many children needed foster parents and what I found truly amazing was the training that was required, especially for special needs children. Darius flashed pictures of children who needed homes. As these sweet faces of children, children of all colors, children of all types of needs flashed on the screen, tears were rolling down my cheeks. Why don't more people know about these children? Why don't people know about this organization? If I was thirty years younger, I would certainly consider opening my heart and home to a foster child.

The Children's Home Society of North Carolina was founded in 1902 in Greensboro, North Carolina. Greensboro at that time was a small agricultural town. A group of businessmen, Young Businessman's Club of Greensboro which is now the Chamber of Commerce, saw the need to do something for homeless children. Simply, their mission was "to provide a home for the child who needs a home and a child for the home which needs a child."

After World War II there was the baby boom. From around 1930 to 1970, The Children's Home Society began placing infants for adoption. At that time the primary purpose was to find homes for newborns with families whose backgrounds and physical characteristics matched their own. Adoptions were sealed. Also during this time, Children's Home Society was beginning to serve the entire state of North Carolina and opened seven more locations.

The 1980's changed society. There was more drug use. Single parents were making the decision to keep their children which meant fewer newborns available to couples who wanted to adopt.

The population of children was growing. More children were entering through the Departments of Social Services. CHS began preparing for children who were referred that were abused and neglected by DSS to be permanently adopted.

To date, Children's Home Society has provided placement for over 16,000 children to permanent, safe and loving homes to help these children and families thrive. Personally, I have talked to several families who have adopted from Children's Home Society of North Carolina. Each family has said in separate conversations, how pleased they were with the entire process, especially post adoption. One family even commented on how thrilled they were when the child they adopted asked about their biological parents and how to handle the subject.

In a conversation with Matt Anderson, Vice President, Programs and Business Development, Children's Home Society has completed more adoptions in 2019. The opioid epidemic that now faces North Carolina has seen an increase of 40% of children needing homes from 2011 to 2017. With over 700 licensed families in North Carolina who talk to their families, word of mouth, the internet and social media, CHS engages with people inquiring about their services.

When asked about New York states Bill of Rights for Adoptees, allowing adoptees to obtain their original birth certificates effective January 15, 2020, CHS has made the decision not to lead as an advocate to open access of birth certificates in North Carolina. It is their belief CHS is not an effective avenue. Will some coalition come in to play to repeal sealed birth certificates of adoptees in North Carolina? We just don't know.

CHS takes what they do very seriously. The hire the most talented and committed people in their field. Their mission statement, vision, core values and beliefs are practiced daily.

MISSION:
To promote the right of every child to a permanent,
safe and loving family.

VISION:
To be a leader in transforming families and
communities so children can thrive

CORE VALUES:
Compassion – Integrity – Excellence – Innovation

WE BELIEVE:

- In the inherent value and potential of every child.
- A child's potential is best nurtured in a family.
- Investing in children and families is the greatest opportunity to improve our communities
- Our history, scope, and expertise call us to leadership on issues affecting children and families.

This is what the Children's Home Society of North Carolina practices every day. Further, CHS believes children need to grow up in their family of origin. When that is not possible, children should grow up in a family of unconditional love. It is also their belief not to separate siblings.

Chapter 17

$\sim\!\!\!\sim$

THE STORK IS COMING!

IT'S AMAZING HOW the subject of adoption comes up in conversation. For some strange reason people are compelled to come up and start a conversation with me. It happens quite frequently. I'm not sure why, but I'm pretty sure God has his hand in it. Has God given me some purpose for complete strangers to approach me? Do I just happen to have an honest face? I'm not quite sure why. Most of the time conversations will circle back to adoption. Sometimes they talk about their own adoption and how they are looking for lost family members. Sometimes they talk about how they are helping a loved one find lost family members. It seems these amazing people have some type of adoption story they want to share with me. I'm very moved to hear these stories. Some of them are beautiful stories which fill my heart with joy. Some stories move me to tears. One thing for sure, all these conversations end up with a hug. I consider all these conversations a gift from God.

Some of the information and findings from 23andMe.com I have received from testing makes a lot of sense and answers many questions

I have had throughout my life. Here's one of the findings 23andMe.com research revealed about me.

"Based on your genetics and other factors, you are less likely to have a fear of public speaking."

"Scientists at 23andMe.com identified 802 genetic markers that are associated with a fear of public speaking. In addition to genetics, other factors like age, sex and ancestry can also influence your chances."

"Of people with genetics and other factors like yours, we predict:

57% do not have a fear of public speaking.

43% have a fear of public speaking."

There is one particular story I feel very compelled to tell you my dear reader. I was asked to speak to a local Rotary Club meeting. I was honored to do so. At first I felt a little nervous. That same day I decided to take a look at my 23andMe account to see if there was anything new. Are there new matches? What health or other genetic findings have come up? Low and behold, information about public speaking came up in my account. I had to laugh. I thought the irony of timing was divine intervention.

Of course, my topic focused on my 50 years plus of my adoption journey. How does one sum up 50 years into 20 minutes of time allowed to speak? I sat down in front of my computer and the words just flowed. I read it to my husband. I think he was a little blown away because I believe there was a little tear in his eye.

The day came to deliver my story. I was escorted to the head table and introduced to the president of the organization. Everyone was very kind and anxious to hear my story. The president presented me with a book to sign. The book, Swabbed & Found, written by Frank Billingsley had a beautiful label inside. I was asked to sign it. The book would be donated to the local library in my honor. This touched my heart.

The time came to deliver my presentation. As I stood in front of the microphone I could feel my heart racing. I gazed around the room and took a deep breath. The room was silent. I was about to begin a presentation to local business leaders.

The words began to flow. I felt very confident in delivering my presentation. Everyone seemed to be listening. Since this was a very personal story about myself everyone in the room seemed to be listening intently. Before I knew it, I had finished my presentation and got an ovation. WOW. I felt God had truly blessed me. Several members asked questions. The meeting was soon adjourned. I hadn't even got out of my seat and many members came up to me. Some asked questions about how to get started and some had shared stories about their adoption. I had handouts that I felt would help those who asked questions. But there was one particular story that touched my heart.

A gentleman came up to me. He had tears in his eyes. He told me how wonderful my presentation was. He proceeded to tell me about he and his wife had adopted a daughter over 30 years ago from Children's Home Society, the very organization I am an ambassador for. I could tell he was a little embarrassed because he was so emotional. I grabbed his hand and said "God's got you". I gave him my contact information and told him I would love to hear more about his family's story. Something told me his story was going to be beautiful. I was really praying he would contact me.

I got in my car. I had not even put the key in the ignition and my cell phone rang. I didn't recognize the number. I usually don't answer my phone unless I recognize my number. But I did and I'm glad I did. It was a gentleman who had been to my presentation and wanted me to be a guest on his television show. We agreed on a date and time. I could feel God's hand working through me. My message of faith, hope and perseverance was being heard.

On the drive home, my phone would ping telling me I had an email. In fact it did it several times. When I got home I immediately checked my email. And there it was…Phil had emailed me. His email was brief but to the point. It was about how he and his wife adopted their daughter Maranda over 30 years ago and how she facilitated a meeting with her biological mother. That in itself is amazing to me but after further reading Phil explained how he and his wife Susan supported her decision to do so. My mind was reeling. I wanted to know more about their story. After carefully thinking of how to respond, I wrote back and asked him if he and his wife would be willing to talk more about their experience in more detail and if I could include their story in this book. They were elated. We agreed to meet at their home a few days later.

I arrived at Phil and Susan's home right on time. I was immediately greeted by Phil and Susan with big smiles and lots of hugs. I was shown pictures of Maranda. She was in her 30's and lives about an hour away and was in training for an upcoming sporting event so she was unable to attend. Both Phil and Susan are very well educated and had both retired from very prominent professions.

Phil and Susan began by saying they were unable to have children of their own. I was immediately drawn into their story as my parents were unable to have children of their own as well. They truly wanted a child, a child to love, a child to make their family complete. Anyone could see Phil and Susan would make amazing parents. They explained how they worked through Children's Home Society. They filled out all the paperwork and went through the home study process. And they waited.....and waited! During their wait Phil and Susan were told to go ahead and get the crib assembled. They didn't buy any baby clothes because they didn't know whether to get clothes for a boy or a girl. Then the call they had been anxiously waiting for finally came. Susan received a call saying that a baby girl had been born. She was elated! Susan then called Phil and said "the stork is coming, the stork is coming" and that he needed to come home immediately to pack and get the paperwork from "the stork", pick up a few outfits at the store then go to get their baby girl. As they were relaying their story to me, I could tell that even to this day they were still elated. I could see their eyes sparkle as they looked at each other while sharing this joyous story with me. The drive was over an hour to the hospital. Phil and Susan's dream was finally coming true. An infant baby girl was going to complete their family.

When Phil and Susan arrived home with their sweet new baby Maranda they were greeted by family who welcomed them home. They were thrilled. Maranda was just a few days old.

Maranda thrived in her new home with her parents. Growing up she had every opportunity available to her. She was able to go college and pursue a wonderful career working with animals. Phil and Susan love her very much. At age five Maranda was told she was adopted. Her parents had been reading her bedtime stories about adoption, puppies were adopted, kittens were adopted and even children were adopted. Maranda loved this story. In fact, Phil and Susan still have the storybook packed away with other treasured memories.

It's very clear to see how much love Phil and Susan have for Maranda. When they talk about her there's always a smile on their face and an unforgettable sparkle in their eyes.

Several years ago, Maranda asked to talk to her father privately. She told him that he would always be her dad and mom would always be her mother and how much she loves them. She did not want to harm their family relationship in any way. She explained that she had been working with a company to help find her biological parents and wanted Phil and Susan's support. Phil was on board but wanted to talk it over with Susan. Sometimes finding biological family can have heart wrenching endings. Sometimes finding biological family can have amazing endings with beautiful beginnings. After talking with Susan, they agreed wholeheartedly to support Maranda.

Maranda had always been curious about her biological parents and she wanted to meet them. She hired a private investigator to help. Maranda gave the investigator non-identifying information from the Children's Home Society along with an original birth certificate. Her mother did not marry the biological father.

It was about three months later that Maranda found out about her biological parents. They were high school sweethearts. It was decided by the family of Maranda's biological mother not to keep Maranda because she wanted to go to college and so did the father. They were just too young and wanted a better life for their daughter.

The investigator that was hired did find Maranda's biological mother and father and arranged for everyone to meet. Miranda's biological mother lived only an hour away. The biological father did not want any contact with Miranda as his wife recently had a miscarriage. A meeting was scheduled at a restaurant for Maranda to finally meet her biological mother.

The big day for Maranda to meet her biological mother finally came. Maranda wanted Phil and Susan to come as well which they did. During my interview with Phil he told me they really didn't say that much because they wanted the experience to be all for Maranda. They chimed into the conversation when needed. There were many matching characteristics between Maranda and her biological mother. Both did not like different foods on the plate touching each other. It's the little things. But it's the little things that matter and can make you smile. Maranda and her biological mother look so much alike.

Maranda's biological mom explained that she was a senior in high school when Maranda was born. She was not ready to have children. She explained that the birth father had been upset because the biological mother was sent away and he had no choice in the matter. Miranda's biological mom did tell his name but didn't give her any contact information. Maranda and her biological mother kept in touch.

Several years later, Maranda's biological father had divorced his wife and wanted to meet her. It took some time for Maranda to decide if she wanted to meet him. She did not want to be rejected. Eventually Maranda decided to meet him at a public restaurant. At the restaurant he talked about his family and was very apologetic about not wanting to meet her. Maranda understood his reasoning. Maranda's biological father had to pay for his education, was religious but not always religious. He was the youngest of six children in his family. Shortly after Maranda was born he developed a problem with alcohol. Maranda's father did graduate from college and has since stopped drinking.

Maranda's biological father now lives a little closer to her. He has invited her to go fishing and hunting but it hasn't worked out yet. It is believed that Maranda's love of animals comes from her biological father.

Maranda's has met her biological mother's parents as well. Although the meeting was somewhat awkward they were so glad to see how well Maranda had grown up, had many opportunities that she may not have had if the circumstances were different. More importantly, they knew she was loved.

Her biological mom developed a very rare form of cancer. She needed a double lung and heart transplant. During this time Maranda's biological mom developed other complications that required her to have a hysterectomy which was very dangerous in her condition but it had to be done. Unfortunately, a few days after the surgery she died. Maranda was in grad school at the time and was unable to attend the private family service. Maranda and her biological mom had a relationship for twelve years until her death.

This story is very near to my heart. Finding biological family answers many questions adoptees may have even right down to small nuances like food on the plate touching each other. It can explain who you look like, it can explain your talents. It is believed Maranda's love of animals comes from her father. Maranda grew up as a sweet and loving girl just like her biological mother and Susan. Both Phil and Susan will tell you they are joyous and complete.

When I asked Phil and Susan why they chose not to adopt another child, their answer was simply that they didn't want to take away the opportunity for someone else to be able to adopt a child. Now that's love!

Chapter 18

S3419 – Bill of Rights for Adoptees

SINCE 1938, NEW York state law sealed all birth certificates for open and closed adoptions. Birth parents of an adopted child were relieved of all parental duties and all responsibilities of the adopted child. The law did not state that birth parents are promised or implied confidentiality. Once parental rights and surrender papers were signed, confidentiality was not given or promised. The only way an adoptee may have even the slightest chance of getting a copy of their original birth certificate was to go before a judge. A judge may approve only if there was a medical emergency or the judge deemed it necessary. Over the past fifty years adoptees have been fighting for what's rightfully theirs, their original birth certificate.

A lobbying organization has recently changed all that. Unsealed Initiative, led by lobbyist Joyce Bahr has recently been instrumental in repealing this archaic law. Unsealed Initiative was founded in 2005. Before that, they had only lobbied once a year and realized people in Albany were not taking it seriously. Joyce had the opportunity to speak to an adopted woman who was in legislature and advised her that she needed to be at the capital more to get the attention they needed.

Joyce began meeting with legislatures and did follow up calls with people she had met with. There's no manual to follow to "get the job done." During Unsealed Initiative's first year, Joyce did everything herself. She'd schedule appointments, made photocopies, put together lobby packets, and did more follow up calls. Joyce Bahr was dedicated to putting Unsealed Initiative on the map. She was driven! Unsealed Initiative began to get sponsors for the bill. Advocates began to realize what she was doing. Being totally dedicated, Joyce never gave up.

In 2005, Unsealed Initiative's legislation was moved out of the Judiciary Committee where Helene Weinstein had tabled it for thirteen years without any discussion. With the help of Chief of Staff John Joyce, the legislation was moved to the Health Committee. Joyce and her team had the opportunity to start lobbying at the capital in Albany while gaining more sponsors for the bill.

For several years, there were ups and downs on getting legislation passed. Momentum was gaining strength as adoption agencies and child welfare organizations were supporting Unsealed Initiative. In 2010, Brooklyn Senator Velmanette Montgomery became the prime sponsor of adoptee rights legislation. However, she was prime sponsor for only one year as she lost her bid for re-election. Staten Island Senator Andrew Lanza stepped up and took over as prime sponsor.

In 2019, democrats took control of the senate and Senator Montgomery became prime sponsor again. This lead to more sponsors and more supporters which resulted in Bill S3419 passing in the senate health committee. Finally, on November 14, 2019, Adoptees Bill of Rights S3419 was signed by The Honorable Andrew M. Cuomo, Governor of New York State. Consequently, the Adoptees Bill of Rights S3419 bill was signed in November which is National Adoption Awareness Month. This bill went into law on January 15, 2020.

When I spoke with Ms. Bahr on the phone, I asked her "what is the one thing you would like people to know." Her answer was simply "Once you get going and you overcome obstacles, even the smallest things matter. Never give up." These words ring so true. Ms. Bahr is living proof.

Adoptees Bill of Rights bill S3419 establishes the right of adoptees to receive an original certified copy of their birth certificate upon reaching the age of 18, or if the adopted person is deceased, the adopted person's direct line descendants, or the lawful representative of such adopted person, or lawful representatives of such deceased adopted person's direct line descendants.

The New York Adoptee Rights Coalition (NYARC) is another key component to getting S3419 signed into law. This coalition not only involves New York but also the strength of many national organizations. This is another organization that has worked tirelessly day in and day out by meeting with legislators, strategizing, and advocating for adoptees to access their original birth certificates.

To me, this means adoptees will finally have new beginnings and resolution. This is our right. Let's hope other states will follow their lead so other adoptees will have their new beginnings and resolution too. DNA has nothing to do with this bill. It just means that New York State adoptees have the legal right to an original birth certificate.

To these organizations and the many others who have devoted their time and energy, I thank you. If you would like to thank the sponsors of this bill, contact information is provided below:

The Honorable Andrew M. Cuomo
Governor of New York State
NYS State Capital Building
Albany, New York, 12224

Phone: 518-474-8390
Office Hours 9:00am to 5:00pm

Senator Velmanette Montgomery
DISTRICT OFFICE
30 Third Avenue
Suite 207
Brooklyn, NY 11217

Phone: 718-643-6140

ALBANY OFFICE
188 State Street
915 Legislative Office Building
Albany, NY 12247

Phone: 518-455-3451

Assemblyman David I. Weprin
DISTRICT OFFICE
185-06 Union Turnpike
Fresh Meadows, NY 11366

Phone: 718-454-3027

DISTRICT OFFICE
111-12 Atlantic Ave., #5
Richmond Hill, NY 11419

Phone: 718-805-2381

ALBANY OFFICE
LOB 526
Albany, NY 12248

Phone: 518-455-5806

Here is information on obtaining an original birth certificate by state. Be sure to check your state of where you were born for any updates.

ALABAMA - Access to Original Birth Certificate Citation: Ala. Code § 22-9A-12(c)-(d) Any person age 19 or older who was born in Alabama and who has had an original birth certificate removed from the files due to an adoption may, upon written request, receive a copy of that birth certificate and any evidence of the adoption held with the original record. A birth parent at any time may request from the State Registrar of Vital Statistics a contact preference form that shall accompany a birth certificate. The contact preference form shall indicate one of the following: • He or she would like to be contacted. • He or she would prefer to be contacted only through an intermediary. • He or she would prefer not to be contacted at this time, but may submit an updated contact preference at a later time. A medical history form shall be supplied to the birth parent upon request of a contact preference form. The medical history form and the contact preference form are confidential communications from the birth parent to the person named on the sealed birth certificate and shall be placed in a sealed envelope upon receipt from the birth parent. The sealed envelope shall be released to a person requesting his or her own original birth certificate. Where the Information Can Be Located • Alabama Department of Public Health, Birth Certificates • The licensed investigating agency appointed by the court per § 26-10A-19(b), (c)

ALASKA - Access to Original Birth Certificate Citation: Alaska Code § 18.50.500 After receiving a request for the identity of a birth parent by an adopted person who is age 18 or older, the State Registrar shall provide the person with an uncertified copy of the person's original birth certificate and any changes in the birth parent's name or address attached to the certificate. An adopted person age 18 or older or a birth parent may submit to the State registrar a notice of change of name or address. The State registrar shall attach the information to the original birth certificate of the adopted person. Where the Information Can Be Located Bureau of Vital Statistics, Alaska Department of Health and Social Services

ARIZONA - Access to Original Birth Certificate Citation: Rev. Stat. § 36-337 The original birth certificate can be made available only upon a court order or as prescribed by rule. Where the Information Can Be Located Arizona Confidential Intermediary Program, Arizona Supreme Court

ARKANSAS - Access to Original Birth Certificate Citation: Ann. Code § 20-18-406 The original birth certificate is available only upon a court order or as provided by regulation. Where the Information Can Be Located • Arkansas Mutual Consent Voluntary Adoption Registry • The licensed agency involved in the adoption

CALIFORNIA - Access to Original Birth Certificate Citation: Health & Safety Code § 102705. The original birth certificate is available only by order of the court. Where the Information Can Be Located • California Department of Social Services • The licensed agency involved in the adoption

COLORADO - Access to Original Birth Certificate Citation: Rev. Stat. § 19-5-305 The option on the contact preference form that allows a birth parent to authorize or not authorize the release of the original birth certificate to eligible parties expires on January 1, 2016. On and after January 1, 2016, contact preference forms shall only address a birth parent's preferences regarding contact and to submit or update medical history. On and after July 1, 2014, the State registrar shall post a notice on its website stating that the contact preference form will be revised to eliminate that option and that birth parents may exercise this option prior to January 1, 2016. Prior to allowing access to an original birth certificate, the State registrar must search for a contact preference form executed prior to January 1, 2016 to ascertain if either birth parent had stated a preference authorizing or not authorizing the release of the original birth certificate. If both birth parents have filed a contact preference form executed prior to January 1, 2016, authorizing the release of the original birth certificate, then the State registrar must release the original birth certificate to the eligible party. If there is no contact preference form on file, or if a contact preference form executed prior to January 1, 2016, is on file stating that the original birth certificate not be released, then the State registrar may not release the original birth certificate prior to January 1, 2016, unless the birth parent rescinds the contact preference form, upon mutual consent of two or more reunited parties, the birth parent is deceased, or the eligible party obtains a court order pursuant to § 19-1-309. When one birth parent has authorized the release of the birth certificate and the other birth parent has filed a contact preference form, prior to January 1, 2016, not authorizing release, the State registrar shall issue the original birth certificate to the eligible party with the name of the nonconsenting parent redacted. Where the Information Can Be Located • Colorado Department of Public Health and Environment • Colorado Intermediary Services • The child-placing agency involved in the adoption

CONNECTICUT - Access to Original Birth Certificate Citation: Ann. Stat. § 7-53 Upon request, the Department of Public Health shall issue an uncertified copy of an original certificate of birth to: • An adopted person who is age 18 or older whose adoption was finalized on or after October 1, 1983 • An adopted person's adult child or grandchild The certificate shall be marked with a notation by the issuer that the original certificate of birth has been superseded by a replacement certificate of birth as on file. Additionally, a notice shall be printed on such certificate or attached thereto stating that information related to the birth parents' preferences regarding contact by the adopted person or the adopted person's adult child or grandchild and a medical health history form completed by the birth parent may be on file with the Department of Children and Families. Where the Information Can Be Located • Connecticut Department of Children and Families • The department and each child-placing agency involved in the adoption

DELAWARE - Access to Original Birth Certificate Citation: Ann. Code Tit. 13, § 923 An adopted person who is age 21 or older may request a copy of the original birth certificate unless the birth parent has filed an affidavit denying release of identifying information. Where the Information Can Be Located • Delaware Office of Vital Statistics • The agency involved in the adoption

DISTRICT OF COLUMBIA - Access to Original Birth Certificate Citation: Ann. Code § 16-314 The original birth certificate is a sealed record that cannot be opened without order of the court. Where the Information Can Be Located • District of Columbia Child and Family Services Agency • The agency involved in the adoption

FLORIDA - Access to Original Birth Certificate Citation: Ann. Stat. § 63.162 The original birth certificate is available only upon order of the court. Where the Information Can Be Located Florida Adoption Reunion Registry, Florida Department of Children and Families

GEORGIA - Access to Original Birth Certificate Citation: Ann. Code § 31-10-14 The original birth certificate is accessible only by order of the court or as provided by statute. Where the Information Can Be Located Georgia Adoption Reunion Registry

GUAM - Access to Original Birth Certificate Citation: Ann. Code Tit. 10, § 3215 The original birth certificate is accessible only upon order of the court. Where the Information Can Be Located The court that approved the adoption

HAWAII - Access to Original Birth Certificate Citation: Rev. Stat. §§ 578-14; 578-15; 338-20 If a new birth certificate is issued, the original birth certificate shall be sealed. The sealed document may be opened by the department only by an order of a court or when requested in accordance with § 578-15. The birth parent may be provided a copy of the original birth certificate upon request. Where the Information Can Be Located Family Court Central Registry

IDAHO - Access to Original Birth Certificate Citation: Ann. Code § 39-258 The original birth certificate is available upon a court order or, in accordance with § 39-259A, when all parties have consented through the State adoption registry. Where the Information Can Be Located Idaho Voluntary Adoption Registry, Vital Records Section, Bureau of Vital Records and Health Statistics

ILLINOIS - Access to Original Birth Certificate Citation: Comp. Stat. Ch. 750, § 50/18.1b Any adopted person who was born in Illinois prior to January 1, 1946, may file with the Illinois Adoption Registry a request for a noncertified copy of an original birth certificate. The registry shall provide the adopted person with an unaltered, noncertified copy of his or her original birth certificate upon receipt of the request. In cases in which an adopted person born prior to January 1, 1946, is deceased, and one of his or her surviving adult children, adult grandchildren, or spouse has registered with the registry, he or she may complete and file with the registry a request for a copy of the birth certificate. The registry shall provide such surviving adult child, adult grandchild, or spouse with an unaltered, noncertified copy of the adopted person's original birth certificate upon receipt of the request. Beginning November 15, 2011, any adult adopted person who was born in Illinois on or after January 1, 1946, may file with the registry a request for a noncertified copy of an original birth certificate. In cases in which the adopted person is deceased, his or her surviving adult child, adult grandchild, or spouse who has registered with the registry may request a noncertified copy of the original birth certificate. If the registry confirms that a requesting adult adopted person, the parent of a requesting adult child of a deceased adopted person, or the husband or wife of a requesting surviving spouse was not the object of a Denial of Information Exchange filed by a birth parent on or before January 1, 2011, and that no birth parent named on the original birth certificate has filed a Birth Parent Preference Form where Option E (prohibiting the release of identifying information) was selected prior to the receipt of a request for an original birth certificate, the registry shall provide the adult adopted person or his or her surviving adult child or spouse with an unaltered noncertified copy of the adopted person's original birth certificate. Where the Information Can Be Located • Illinois Adoption Registry, Illinois Department of Public Health • Confidential Intermediary Service of Illinois, Midwest Adoption Center (MAC)

INDIANA - Access to Original Birth Certificate Citation: Ann. Stat. § 31-19-13-2 The original birth certificate is withheld from inspection except for a child adopted by a stepparent or as provided in statutes pertaining to release of identifying information. Where the Information Can Be Located Indiana Adoption History Registry, Indiana State Department of Health, Vital Statistics

IOWA - Access to Original Birth Certificate Citation: Ann. Stat. § 144.24 The original birth certificate may not be inspected except under order of a court. The State Registrar shall, upon the application of an adult adopted person, a birth parent, an adoptive parent, or the legal representative of the any of the former, inspect the original birth certificate and reveal to the applicant the date of the adoption and the name and address of the court that issued the adoption decree. Where the Information Can Be Located Iowa Mutual Consent Voluntary Adoption Registry, Iowa Department of Public Health, Bureau of Vital Records

KANSAS - Access to Original Birth Certificate Citation: Ann. Stat. § 65-2423 The original birth certificate is a sealed document that may be opened by the State Registrar only upon the demand of the adult adopted person or by an order of the court. Where the Information Can Be Located Kansas Department for Children and Family Services, Post Adoption Search and Records

KENTUCKY - Access to Original Birth Certificate Citation: Rev. Stat. § 199.570 The original birth certificate is available only upon court order. Where the Information Can Be Located Kentucky Cabinet for Families and Children

LOUISIANA - Access to Original Birth Certificate Citation: Rev. Stat. § 40:73 The original birth certificate is available: • Upon court order to the adopted person, or if deceased, the adopted person's descendants, or the adoptive parent • To the agency that was a party to the adoption upon court order after a showing of compelling reasons. Where the Information Can Be Located Louisiana Voluntary Adoption Registry, Department of Children and Family Services

MAINE - Access to Original Birth Certificate Citation: Rev. Stat. Tit. 22, §§ 2765; 2768 The original certificate of birth is not subject to inspection except upon order of the court or pursuant to § 2768. An adopted person, his or her attorney, or, if the adopted person is deceased, his or her descendants may obtain a copy of that person's original certificate of birth from the State Registrar of Vital Statistics. The adopted person must be at least age 18 and have been born in this State. The adopted person must file a written application and provide appropriate proof of identification to the State Registrar. Upon receipt of the written application and proof of identification and fulfillment of the requirements listed below, the State Registrar shall issue a noncertified copy of the unaltered original certificate of birth to the applicant. The State Registrar may require a waiting period and impose a fee for the noncertified copy. The fees and waiting period imposed under this subsection must be identical to the fees and waiting period generally imposed on persons seeking their own birth certificates. If a contact preference or medical history form has been completed and submitted to the State Registrar pursuant to § 2769, the State Registrar also must provide that information. Where the Information Can Be Located Maine State Adoption Reunion Registry, Office of Vital Records

MARYLAND - Access to Original Birth Certificate Citation: Fam. Law §§ 5-359; 5-3A-42; 5-3B-29 For adoptions finalized on or after January 1, 2000: • An adopted person who is at least age 21 may apply to the secretary for a copy of his or her original birth certificate. • If an adopted person is at least age 21, a birth parent may apply to the secretary for a copy of the adopted person's original birth certificate. A birth parent may file with the director a disclosure veto to bar disclosure of information about that parent in an accessible record. The birth parent may also cancel a disclosure veto and refile a disclosure veto at any time. An adult adopted person may file a disclosure veto to bar disclosure of information about him or her in an accessible record. The adopted person may also cancel a disclosure veto and refile a disclosure veto at any time. Except as provided below, the secretary shall give to each applicant who meets the requirements of this section a copy of each record that the applicant requested and that the secretary has on file. Whenever a birth parent applies for a record, the secretary shall redact from the copy all information as to: • The other birth parent if that parent has filed a disclosure veto • The adopted person and each adoptive parent if the adopted person has filed a disclosure veto. Whenever an adopted person applies for a record, the secretary shall redact from the copy all information as to the birth parent if that parent has filed a disclosure veto. Where the Information Can Be Located Mutual Consent Voluntary Adoption Registry, Maryland Social Services Administration

MASSACHUSETTS - Access to Original Birth Certificate Citation: Ann. Laws Ch. 210, § 5C All records concerning the adoption proceedings are available only upon court order. Where the Information Can Be Located Adoption Search Coordinator, Massachusetts Department of Social Services

MICHIGAN - Access to Original Birth Certificate Citation: Comp. Laws § 333.2882 A copy of the original birth certificate may be provided to the adult adopted person upon request when accompanied by a copy of a central adoption registry clearance reply form or by court order. Where the Information Can Be Located Michigan Confidential Intermediary Program, Michigan Department of Human Services

MINNESOTA - Access to Original Birth Certificate Citation: Ann. Stat. § 259.89 An adopted person who is age 19 or older may request the Commissioner of Health to disclose the information on his or her original birth record. Within 5 days, the commissioner shall notify the Department of Human Services or child-placing agency of the request. Within 6 months after receiving the request, the department or agency shall make reasonable efforts to notify each birth parent. If the department is unable to notify a parent identified on the original birth record within 6 months, and if neither parent has at any time filed an unrevoked consent to disclosure, the information may be disclosed as follows: • If the person was adopted prior to August 1, 1977, he or she may petition the court for disclosure, and the court shall grant the petition if, after consideration of the interests of all known persons involved, the court determines that disclosure of the information would be of greater benefit than nondisclosure. • If the person was adopted on or after August 1, 1977, the commissioner shall release the information to the adopted person. If either birth parent has ever filed with the commissioner an unrevoked affidavit stating that the information on the original birth record should not be disclosed, the commissioner shall not disclose the information until the affidavit is revoked by the filing of a consent to disclosure by that parent. If a parent named on the original birth record has died, and at any time prior to the death the parent has filed an unrevoked affidavit stating that the information not be disclosed, the adopted person may petition the court of original jurisdiction of the adoption proceeding for disclosure. The State Registrar shall provide a copy of an adopted person's original birth record to an authorized representative of a federally recognized American Indian Tribe for the sole purpose of determining the adopted person's eligibility for enrollment or membership in the Tribe. Where the Information Can Be Located Adoption Archive, Minnesota Department of Health (Child Safety and Permanency Division, Adoption Assistance Program)

MISSISSIPPI - Access to Original Birth Certificate Citation: Ann. Code §§ 93-17-21; 93-17-205. The original birth certificate shall not be a public record and shall not be divulged except upon the order of the court or pursuant to §§ 93-17-201 through 93-17-223. The birth parent may file with the bureau at any time an affidavit authorizing the bureau to provide the adopted person with his or her original birth certificate, or an affidavit expressly prohibiting the release of any information. The affidavit may be revoked at any time by written notification to the bureau. Where the Information Can Be Located • Mississippi Department of Health, Vital Records • The licensed agency involved in the adoption

MISSOURI - Access to Original Birth Certificate Citation: Ann. Stat. § 193.125 The State Registrar shall file the original certificate of birth with the certificate of decree of adoption and such file may be opened by the State Registrar only upon receipt of a certified copy of an order as decreed by the court of adoption. Where the Information Can Be Located Missouri Division of Family Services, Adoption Information Registry

MONTANA - Access to Original Birth Certificate Citation: Ann. Code § 42-6-109 In addition to any copy of an adopted person's original birth certificate authorized for release by a court order issued pursuant to § 50-15-121 or 50-15-122, the department shall furnish a copy of the original birth certificate of an adopted person: • Upon the written request of a person who was adopted before October 1, 1985, or 30 years or more ago, whichever date is later • Upon a court order for a person adopted on or after October 1, 1985, and before October 1, 1997 • For a person adopted on or after October 1, 1997, upon: » The written request of an adopted person who has reached age 18 unless the birth parent has requested in writing that the original birth certificate not be automatically released » A court order

NEBRASKA - Access to Original Birth Certificate Citation: Rev. Stat. §§ 43-130; 43-136; 43-143; 43-146.04 For adoptions finalized prior to September 1, 1998, an adopted person who is age 25 or older may file a written request for the original birth certificate. For adoptions finalized on or after September 1, 1998, an adopted person who is age 21 or older may request the original birth certificate. If a consent form has been signed and filed by both birth parents, or by the birth mother of a child born out of wedlock, and no nonconsent form has been filed, a copy of the adopted person's original birth certificate shall be provided to the adopted person. For adoptions finalized prior to July 20, 2002, an adoptive parent or parents may at any time file a notice of nonconsent stating that at no time prior to his or her death, or the death of both parents if each signed the form, may any information on the adopted person's original birth certificate be released to such adopted person. Where the Information Can Be Located Nebraska Department of Health and Human Services, Division of Children and Family Services—Adoption Searches

NEVADA - Access to Original Birth Certificate Citation: Rev. Stat. § 440.310 The original birth certificate is available only upon order of the court. Where the Information Can Be Located Nevada Adoption Registry Services, Division of Child and Family Services

NEW HAMPSHIRE - Access to Original Birth Certificate Citation: Rev. Stat. § 170:B-23 The original birth certificate is subject to inspection only upon written order of the court for good cause shown. Where the Information Can Be Located New Hampshire Department of State, Division of Vital Records

NEW JERSEY - Access to Original Birth Certificate Citation: Ann. Stat. §§ 26:8-40.1; 26:8-40.33 Effective until January 1, 2017: The State Registrar shall place under seal the original certificate of birth and all papers pertaining to the new certificate of birth. The seal shall not be broken except by order of a court of competent jurisdiction. Effective January 1, 2017: Upon receipt of a request pursuant to § 26:8-40.1(c), the State Registrar shall provide the authorized requester with an uncertified, long-form copy of the adopted person's original certificate of birth. Where the Information Can Be Located New Jersey Department of Children and Families, Adoption Registry

NEW MEXICO - Access to Original Birth Certificate Citation: Ann. Stat. § 24-14-17 The original birth certificate is available only upon order of the court. Where the Information Can Be Located New Mexico Adoption Search, Department of Children, Youth and Families

***NEW YORK** – Original Birth Certificates will be available January 15, 2020

NORTH CAROLINA - Access to Original Birth Certificate Citation: Gen. Stat. § 48-9-106 Upon receipt of a certified copy of a court order issued pursuant to § 48-9-105 authorizing the release of an adopted person's original birth certificate, the State Registrar shall give the individual who obtained the order a copy of the original birth certificate with a certification that the copy is a true copy of a record that is no longer a valid certificate of birth. Where the Information Can Be Located North Carolina Department of Health and Human Services, Division of Social Services

NORTH DAKOTA - Access to Original Birth Certificate Citation: Cent. Code § 23-02.1-18 The original birth record is available only upon order of a court or as provided by rules and regulations. Where the Information Can Be Located North Dakota Department of Human Services, Adoption Search/Disclosure

OHIO - Access to Original Birth Certificate Citation: Rev. Code §§ 3705.12; 3705.126 Upon the issuance of the new birth record, the original birth record shall cease to be a public record. The department shall place the original birth record and the items sent by the probate court pursuant to § 3107.19 in an adoption file and seal the file. The contents of the adoption file are not a public record and shall be available only in accordance with § 3705.126. The contents of the adoption file include any contact preference form, birth parent's name redaction request form, or social and medical history accepted and maintained by the department. The department shall neither open an adoption file nor make its contents available except as follows: • The department shall inspect the file to determine the court involved. • The department shall make the file's contents available to an adopted person or lineal descendant of an adopted person in accordance with § 3107.38. • The department shall open the file to transfer releases to the file in accordance with § 3107.381. • The department shall open the file to file a contact preference form from a birth parent and remove any previously filed contact preference form from the birth parent. • The department shall open the file to file a birth parent's name redaction request form or to remove and destroy the form. • The department shall open the file to file a denial of release form or an authorization of release form. • The department shall make the file's contents available to an adopted person or adoptive parent in accordance with § 3107.47. • The department shall open the file to file a request from an adopted person under § 3107.48 or to remove and destroy the request. • The department shall inspect the file to assist a birth parent or birth sibling in finding the adopted person's name by adoption in accordance with § 3107.49. • The court that decreed the adoption may order that the contents be made open for inspection or available for copying. Where the Information Can Be Located Ohio Department of Health, Adoption Information

OKLAHOMA - Access to Original Birth Certificate Citation: Ann. Stat. Tit. 10, § 7505-6.6 For adoptions finalized after November 1, 1997, an uncertified copy of the original birth certificate is available to an adopted person, age 18 or older, upon written request under the following conditions: • He or she presents proof of identity. • There are no birth siblings under age 18 who are currently in an adoptive family and whose whereabouts are known. • The birth parents have not filed affidavits of nondisclosure. Original birth certificates are also available upon order of the court for good cause shown, pursuant to § 7505-1.1. Where the Information Can Be Located • Adoption Reunion Registry, Oklahoma Department of Human Services • Confidential Intermediary Search Program, Oklahoma Department of Human Services

OREGON - Access to Original Birth Certificate Citation: Ann. Stat. § 432.228 Upon receipt of a written application to the State Registrar, any adopted person age 21 and older born in the State of Oregon shall be issued a certified copy of his or her unaltered, original, and un-amended certificate of birth that is in the custody of the State Registrar, with procedures, filing fees, and waiting periods identical to those imposed upon non adopted citizens. A birth parent may at any time request from the State Registrar of the Center for Health Statistics or from a voluntary adoption registry a contact preference form that shall accompany a birth certificate issued under the section above. The contact preference form shall provide the following information, to be completed at the option of the birth parent: • I would like to be contacted. • I would prefer to be contacted only through an intermediary. • I prefer not to be contacted at this time. If I decide later that I would like to be contacted, I will register with the voluntary adoption registry. I have completed an updated medical history and have filed it with the voluntary adoption registry. The certificate from the voluntary adoption registry verifying receipt of an updated medical history shall be in a form prescribed by the Oregon Health Authority and shall be supplied upon request of the birth parent by the voluntary adoption registry. When the State Registrar receives a completed contact preference form from a birth parent, the State Registrar shall match the contact preference form with the adopted person's sealed file. The contact preference form shall be placed in the adopted person's sealed file when a match is made. A completed contact preference form shall be confidential. Where the Information Can Be Located Oregon Department of Human Services, Adoption Search and Registry Program

PENNSYLVANIA - Access to Original Birth Certificate Citation: Cons. Stat. Tit. 23, § 2937 No disclosure shall be made regarding an adopted person's original birth record or regarding the documents or proof on which an amended certificate of birth is based or relating in any way to the birth parents unless the disclosure is made pursuant to the provisions of this section. The birth parents may, at the time their parental rights are terminated or at any time thereafter, place on file with the court and the Department of Health a consent form granting permission for the court or the department to issue a copy of the summary of the adopted person's original birth record, disclosing the identity of the birth parents, at any time after the adopted person turns age 18 or, if the adopted person is younger than age 18, to the adoptive parent or legal guardian. If only one birth parent has filed a consent, a copy of the summary of the original birth record naming only the consenting birth parent shall be issued. The consent of a birth parent may be withdrawn at any time by filing a withdrawal of consent form with the court and the Department of Health. Where the Information Can Be Located Pennsylvania Department of Health, Adoption Information Registry

PUERTO RICO - Access to Original Birth Certificate Citation: Ann. Laws Tit. 24, § 1136 The original birth certificate is available only upon order of the court. Where the Information Can Be Located Vital Statistics Registry

RHODE ISLAND - Access to Original Birth Certificate Citation: Gen. Laws § 15-7.2-12 In the event of a verified match and release of identifying information, the registry, upon the written request of the adult adopted person, shall certify to the State Registrar of Vital Records that the adult adopted person is a party to a verified match and is entitled to receive uncertified copies of his or her original birth certificate. The certification shall also state that no person other than the adult adopted person is entitled to receive copies of the original birth certificate. However, no uncertified copy of the original birth certificate may be released to the adult adopted person unless each party named on the original birth certificate has registered. Registration by a birth parent not named on the original birth certificate shall not be required for release of the uncertified copy of the original birth certificate.

SOUTH CAROLINA - Access to Original Birth Certificate Citation: Ann. Code § 44-63-140 The original birth certificate is placed in a special sealed file by the State Registrar. The statute does not specify a procedure for access to the original certificate. Where the Information Can Be Located Adoption Reunion Registry, South Carolina Department of Social Services

SOUTH DAKOTA - Access to Original Birth Certificate Citation: Ann. Code § 34-25-16.4 The original birth certificate is available upon order of the court. Where the Information Can Be Located South Dakota Department of Social Services, Adoption Registry

TENNESSEE - Access to Original Birth Certificate Citation: Ann. Code § 36-1-130 The original birth certificate is available to parties who have established their eligibility to have access to adoption records. Where the Information Can Be Located Tennessee Department of Children's Services, Advance Notice Registry

TEXAS - Access to Original Birth Certificate Citation: Health & Safety Code § 192.008 Only the court that granted the adoption may grant access to the original birth certificate. Where the Information Can Be Located Texas Department of State Health Services, Central Adoption Registry

UTAH - Access to Original Birth Certificate Citation: Ann. Code §§ 78B-6-103(3); 78B-6-141 An 'adoption document' is an adoption-related document filed with the office, a petition for adoption, a decree of adoption, an original birth certificate, or evidence submitted in support of a supplementary birth certificate. An adoption document is sealed and may only be open to inspection and copying as follows: • By a party to the adoption proceeding while the proceeding is pending or within 6 months after the adoption decree is entered • When a court enters an order permitting access to the documents by a person who has appealed the denial of that person's motion to intervene • Upon order of the court expressly permitting inspection or copying, after good cause has been shown • As provided under § 78B-6-144 • When the adoption document becomes public on the 100th anniversary of the date the final decree of adoption was entered • When the birth certificate becomes public on the 100th anniversary of the date of birth • To a mature adopted person or a parent who adopted the mature adopted person without a court order, unless the final decree of adoption is entered by the juvenile court • To an adult adopted person, to the extent permitted below

VERMONT - Access to Original Birth Certificate Citation: Ann. Stat. Tit. 15A, § 6-107 The original birth certificate may be released upon request to an adopted person who is age 18 or older and who has access to identifying information. The original birth certificate is unsealed and becomes public record 99 years after the date of the adopted person's birth. Where the Information Can Be Located Vermont Adoption Registry, Department for Children and Families

VIRGIN ISLANDS - Access to Original Birth Certificate Citation: Ann. Code Tit. 16, § 145 The original birth record is not available to anyone other than the adopted person after attaining majority or upon order of the court. Where the Information Can Be Located This issue is not addressed in the statutes reviewed.

VIRGINIA - Access to Original Birth Certificate Citation: Ann. Code § 32.1-261 Upon receipt of notice of a decision or order granting an adult adopted person access to identifying information regarding his or her birth parents from the Commissioner of Social Services or a circuit court, and proof of identification and payment, the State Registrar shall mail an adult adopted person a copy of the original certificate of birth. Where the Information Can Be Located Virginia Department of Social Services, Adoption Unit

WASHINGTON - Access to Original Birth Certificate Citation: Rev. Code § 26.33.345 A noncertified copy of the original birth certificate is available to the birth parent upon request. For adoptions finalized after October 1, 1993, the Department of Health shall provide a noncertified copy of the original birth certificate upon request to an adopted person who is age 18 or older, unless the birth parent has filed an affidavit of nondisclosure before July 28, 2013, or a contact preference form that indicates he or she does not want the original birth certificate released, provided that the affidavit of nondisclosure, the contact preference form, or both have not expired. For adoptions finalized on or before October 1, 1993, the department may not provide a noncertified copy of the original birth certificate to the adopted person until after June 30, 2014. After June 30, 2014, the department shall provide a noncertified copy of the original birth certificate upon request to an adopted person age 18 or older, unless the birth parent has filed a contact preference form that indicates he or she does not want the original birth certificate released, provided that the contact preference form has not expired. An affidavit of nondisclosure expires upon the death of the birth parent. Where the Information Can Be Located Washington State Department Health, Original Birth Certificate for an Adopted Person

WEST VIRGINIA - Access to Original Birth Certificate Citation: Ann. Code § 16-5-18 The State Registrar shall establish a new certificate of birth for a person born in West Virginia when he or she receives a certificate of adoption or a certified copy of the order of adoption, together with the information necessary to identify the original certificate of birth and to establish a new certificate of birth. A new certificate of birth shall show the actual city, county and date of birth, if known, and shall be substituted for the original certificate of birth on file. The original certificate of birth and the evidence of adoption may be inspected only upon order of a court of competent jurisdiction, except as provided by legislative rule or as otherwise provided by State law. Where the Information Can Be Located West Virginia Mutual Consent Voluntary Adoption Registry, Department of Health and Human Resources

WISCONSIN - Access to Original Birth Certificate Citation: Ann. Stat. § 48.433 The original birth certificate is available upon request to the adopted person who is age 21 or older if the birth parents have filed affidavits authorizing disclosure. Where the Information Can Be Located Adoption Records Search Program, Wisconsin Department of Children and Families

WYOMING - Access to Original Birth Certificate Citation: Ann. Stat. § 35-1-417 The original birth certificate is not subject to inspection except by court order. Where the Information Can Be Located Wyoming Department of Family Services, Adoption

This material may be freely reproduced and distributed. However, when doing so, please credit Child Welfare Information Gateway. This publication is available online at https://www.childwelfare.gov/topics/systemwide/laws-policies/statutes/infoaccessap/.

Chapter 19

A Letter to my Adoptive Dad

Dear Dad,

I can't begin to tell you how much I miss talking to you. It was very difficult for all of us to watch you slip away. Dementia is very difficult. I want you to know that I did my best taking care of mom after you passed. Her death took Ann and me by surprise.

Ben and Adam have grown to be amazing dads. Ben has a daughter, Laura who is 7 years old now. Laura loves ballet, T-ball and cheerleading. It's so funny to watch Ben help Laura out by practicing the ballet and cheerleading moves. He recently bought a pop up camper and has given it a complete makeover. I'm so glad they get to go camping and make wonderful memories. Some of our camping trips we did while I was growing up are some of my fondest memories. Remember camping in the Florida Everglades and I you counted over 100 mosquito bites on me? It wasn't fun then but now I can laugh about it.

Adam and Amanda have two children. Adam is an ordained minister and continues his work in Southwest Virginia. Amanda is working on her master's degree in social work. Ella, who was born about three weeks after Laura, loves T-ball and playing piano. She's a very smart girl and can carry on some very interesting conversations. She will start first grade in the fall. And then there's Paul. Dad, he's so funny and he would melt your heart. His middle name is Wesley in memory of you and he just turned four. It's hard to believe I am a grandmother and I am so proud of my grandchildren. I love them with all my heart.

I want to tell you the story of how I met my husband William. Dad, you would really love him. He's an engineer and a good Christian man. I met him in December, 2006. He was playing music at a bar. He was amazing. I asked a friend of mine who he was and she didn't know. My reply was that I wanted to find out. I love his music. He took a short break and came up to me and started talking. He said he had seen me watching him. I must have looked like some kind of geek. LOL. Next thing I know, we discovered we lived in the same apartment complex and we exchanged phone numbers. I didn't think he would call but he did. I went to spend Christmas with you and mom. Ann came down too. Little did we know it would be your last Christmas. That Christmas was the best ever. Mom didn't want to decorate at all. Ann and I wouldn't have that. We went up to the storage locker and dragged out all the Christmas decorations, played Christmas music and you ate a full pound of shrimp, much to mom's chagrin. Despite your dementia, you smiled and we all know how much you enjoyed every bite. Ann and I still talk about that Christmas and how special it was.

After the holiday, Ann and I had to go home. William and I continued seeing each other. It was several months later when you died and I returned to Virginia to help mom. Your memorial service was beautiful. There were lots of people there.

We did our best to take care of mom. I visited as much as possible. William was very understanding of my frequent trips back to Virginia.

It took me some time to figure out how I would carry out your wishes of having your ashes placed in the Blue Ridge Mountains. I talked to William about it and we decided to carry out your wish. I will never ever forget that day. William and I drove to the mountains and hiked up the mountain. It was cold, misting and flat out miserable. We found a beautiful overlook on the trail to the top. I told William this is the place. The view of the mountains was so beautiful. We were both cold, wet and miserable but we persevered. Having never spread anyone's ashes before I asked William how we should do it. He suggested a prayer. So we held hands and said a prayer and released your ashes into the wind. The ashes floated with the wind. Dad, it was so beautiful. It was at that very moment of releasing your ashes that I fell in love with William. It was magic.

We hiked back down the mountain. It was still cold and rainy but my heart was filled with happiness and warmth. You were where you wanted to be. You were finally free. God bless you dad.

It was in July, 2008 when William and I married. It was a beautiful wedding in a small church. Mom was there. It was her last trip she took before she died. I want you to know that William takes good care of me. He's very supportive. He's been very supportive of me finding my biological family.

It wasn't until after mom died that I decided to start searching for them. After an exhausting four years I finally found and met my biological father and three full blood sisters. They are all in upstate New York. I flew to New York in January, 2019 to stay with Ann and meet my biological family. My biological mother is still living but isn't ready to meet me yet. That's ok. Maybe that will change. My biological father is a good man. He's 83 and still works to this day. He's a very tall man and I look just like him. My three sisters are amazing too. We all look alike. I am the oldest sibling. They have accepted me with open arms and hearts.

Ann has also found several half siblings. They too are amazing people. Ann is also the oldest. Her new family and my new family are good people dad. Both Ann's biological mother and biological father are deceased. Ann and I talk all the time. If you and mom had not adopted us our lives would have been very different. We both are blessed to call you dad.

I think of you and mom every day and miss you both but I know where you are and that someday soon we will be together. Sometimes I can almost smell your pipe tobacco and hear your voice.

I also don't want you to think that finding my biological family has changed the way I feel about you and mom. It doesn't! Not one bit! You gave our family such a wonderful life dad. You're a true father and a great Christian man. I am one lucky person to have you and mom as my parents.

I love you.

D.

Chapter 20

———❧———

A Letter to my Adoptive Mom

January, 2020

Dear Mom,

It's been about ten years since you've left this Earth for Heaven. There are so many things I want to tell you. I wish I could have been there holding your hand while you slipped away. It makes me happy that John was there with you. I know how much he meant to you and dad.

I can't imagine what your last minutes here on Earth must have been like? Were you in pain? We're you ready to meet Jesus? Did you realize that it wouldn't be long before you'd be reunited with dad very soon and that all your pain and suffering would be gone? We all find comfort in the fact that you were at peace. Ann and I wish we had known where you were. We tried to find you. You were never a burden to us. We thought you were the glue that held us together.

I miss your smile. I miss your laughter. I miss the notebook of all the jokes you printed out from your email. I miss how you were the "queen" of the computer office. I'm proud you taught yourself how to use the computer later in your life. I miss taking you out to lunch at your favorite restaurant. I love how your neighbors came to see you all the time and the tidbits of gossip you loved to share. Your facial expressions when telling the latest gossip was hysterical.

Let me tell you about your grandsons Ben and Adam. Ben has turned out to be quite a man. He lives in Virginia. He talks about Dad quite a bit. He loves you both so much and wishes you could meet his daughter Laura. She's quite the princess and loves unicorns and the color purple. She takes ballet, she's a cheerleader and likes to play T-ball. It's so funny to watch Ben with her. He knows all the ballet and cheerleading moves. I know you're laughing. In the fall Laura will be starting First grade. I'm so proud of her. Ben and his family just bought a pop up camper. He remodeled the inside and it's gorgeous. They are looking forward to adventures and making memories on camping trips.

Adam and Amanda still live in Southwest Virginia. Adam is now an ordained minister in his church. I can't tell you how proud I am of him. William and I went up for a visit not long ago and I was quite humbled when I received Communion from him. It was a very sacred and emotional moment in life. Amanda is a social worker and going back to school to get her master's degree. These two are so much in love. You can really see it when they look at each other. They know the importance of communication and take their relationship very seriously. Ella is a mini Adam. She will also start First grade in the fall. Ella loves to fly into my arms when she sees me. She's a very tall girl for her age. She's the height of an eight-year old. Her eyes are like Adam's only with the cutest glasses you've ever seen. Ella plays T-Ball and piano. That girl has the gift of gab too. It's like you're talking to an adult. Then there is Paul Wesley. Yes, he is named after Dad. This is just one more proof positive of the influence you and dad had on Adam. He's adorable and very smart for his age. He'll be four very soon. Both Ella and Paul know all about

Jesus. As Ella says, "I'm a preacher's daughter." I just smile and say "yes you are."

Being a grandmother has certainly changed my heart. Its fun to watch them grow, hear them laugh and sometimes we even get into a little mischief together.

These three children would make you laugh, they'd make you crazy but most of all they would adore and love you. I never imagined what it meant to be a grandmother. Now I know.

Since you've been gone, Ann and I have gotten very close. When we cleaned out your apartment we looked for any possible clues surrounding our adoptions. We didn't find anything and that was okay. Of course we both always wondered. Through several conversations over the past few years, we shared bits and pieces of what we knew or thought we knew. About four years ago I told Ann that I had taken a DNA test. DNA testing and technology has changed so much for adoptees and the possibility of connecting with biological family and knowing more about your nationality and even health information. It turned out I am 60% Great British, Irish and Welch and I have amazingly healthy genes. The information was difficult for me to understand and my closest relative was a second cousin.

Here's where the technology kicks in. I belong to several DNA groups on Facebook. I made a comment about my findings and asked for help. A woman by the name of Carol from upstate New York reached out to me and said she could help me. So after many text and email messages we proceeded to the next step which was obtaining my non-identifying information from the state of New York. That process took about six weeks. I sent a copy to Carol and was amazed at what information she could use to help me. After relentless months which turned into years, she found my biological family.

Along the way I would tell Ann about my findings. Ann decided that she too would take a DNA test. She took the DNA test and Carol helped her as well. Two weeks before Christmas, 2018 Carol gave me the name of my biological mother and 3 sisters. She didn't know if my sisters were full siblings or half siblings. Since it was Christmas, I did not reach out to biological family. December 31, 2018, Ann received a call from a half-sister. Her half-sister Gayle was thrilled to find Ann. Ann has quite a few half brothers and sisters. Her biological mother died of cancer. Ann's connection to biological family inspired me to reach out to my biological family.

I chose to reach out to Gina, the youngest sibling. It was the most difficult conversation I have ever had. She was just as shocked as I was. After a while, the conversation got easier and easier. She was going to do a research about it and get back to me. The next day she called me and confirmed everything. Gina and her sister Becky went to their father and confronted him. He said it was true and was excited the truth had finally come out. I not only had a dad but my sisters are full siblings. My biological fathers name is Gerald and my biological mothers name is Marian. They grew up in upstate, NY. Gerald knew about me. Marian was forced by her mother to give me up for adoption since she wasn't married to Gerald. Low and behold, four months after I was born in 1955, Gerald and Marian were married and immediately had Jackie followed by Becky, then Gina. I am the oldest.

I went to upstate New York in January, 2019 to meet not only Ann's siblings but to meet my father and three sisters. Mom, they're good people. I told my father thank you for giving me the precious gift of life. My mother is not ready to meet me. That's okay. I pray she may change her mind. I had put together a photo album and gave it to Gerald. Gerald is 83 years old and still working. And he's very healthy. Everyone has accepted me and we all talk often.

I can only imagine what a beautiful place Heaven must be. I know we will all be together at some point. I think of you and Dad every day and miss you. Ben and Adam talk about you too. Adam still has your Christmas tree you made me way back when and the train that goes around the tree. His children love it. Both Ben and Adam tell their children about you and dad. They share stories about growing up and just how much you and dad influenced them growing up. We all talk about you often. I still find myself picking up the phone to call you. I stop and remember that you are not here. Even though you are not here mom, you are forever in our hearts.

I love you.

D.

Chapter 21

———— ∞ ————

March 6, 2020

As of January 15, 2020, Governor Andrew Cuomo signed into law allowing adoptees from New York State to apply for their pre-adoption birth certificates—Original birth certificate. For those of us born in New York State, this new law S3419 is wonderful. We now have a piece of a puzzle that is rightfully ours.

I had been watching my Facebook DNA groups and reading various posts. Many were thrilled and rushed to order theirs at 11:59 pm on January 14th. It seemed like there were hundreds, maybe even thousands that were anxiously filling out the paperwork and sending in their money to expedite the delivery of their birth certificate. I decided to check out the instructions on the appropriate website and make sure I had all the required information ready at my fingertips when I was ready to apply. It looked to be very cut and dry.

On January 19th, I decided to go ahead and complete my application to get my original birth certificate. I remember my hands actually shaking to the point that I couldn't fill out the form. I took a deep breath and plowed right in. I filled out all the appropriate boxes and payment information then pressed send. In thirty five to forty days my original birth certificate would be arriving at my door by UPS.

I kept reading posts on my Facebook DNA groups that were adoptees from New York State. Some were overjoyed at their newfound information. Their birth certificates gave them answers they had been waiting for for years. I was thrilled for them. Some stories were heartbreaking. Even though I had met my biological father, three full blood sisters, nieces, aunts and uncles, I could feel my anxiety level rise. Who's to say that some new information may pop up? How would I handle it? Time would tell.

On March 5th I received a tracking number from UPS that my package would be arriving the very next day. I stayed home since I had to sign for the delivery. I just kept busy. It was about eleven on the morning of March 6th that my package arrived. The UPS delivery guy was so nice. I told him that this package carried information I had been waiting for all my life. I signed for the package and sat on my couch. Should I open it now? Should I wait to William got home? I chose to wait for William to get home.

When William got home and I was holding the UPS envelope in my hand. He sat down next to me and watched as I opened the envelope. There were two pieces of paper inside. The top paper was my original birth certificate. I could feel the sting of tears in my eyes. I read the information slowly. Some of it was information I already knew from my non-identifying information. But there were three pieces of information that really popped out. First, my biological fathers name was not on the document. This is not unusual since the father's information was not required when the mother was single at the time of the birth. Basically, fathers were not given the opportunity to have their name on the birth certificate. The second piece of new information I received was that I had a name. My given name at birth was Mary. The third piece of new information was the final date of adoption. My adoption was finalized on March 5th which is exactly sixty four years and one day from the date I received this document. God really does have a sense of humor.

Epilogue

I'm a 64 year old adoptee. I don't let my adoption define me. It is however a very big part of my life and very important part of my being. Being an adoptee has made me strong and confident. I look back to when I was much younger and I can now see why my personality is shaped the way it is. As an adoptee, I always felt I needed to be better, I needed to shine. I never wanted to let anyone down for fear of being sent away. But that's one of the traits of being adopted. It's in my DNA.

I was bullied as a teenager because I was adopted. Those who bullied me told me I was not wanted. To those bullies I say their judgmental statement was very wrong. In fact, it's quite the opposite. I was wanted by my adoptive parents and I was loved unconditionally. When I met my biological father for the first time, one of the very first things he told me is that he never wanted to let me go and that he loves me.

Being relinquished at birth isn't such a bad thing. In fact, it's the most generous gift of life and love. My biological mother was the one person really bullied. She was bullied because society said it wasn't acceptable to have a child out of wedlock. Society has come a long way in the acceptance of single women having children.

To say that reuniting with biological family isn't for the faint of heart is an understatement. During my entire journey, so many things could have happened very differently. For example, when I first learned who my sisters and biological mother were, I chose not to make contact. It was Christmas and I certainly did not want to make a call to anyone that would possibly turn their holiday upside down much less their lives. Waiting for the right time to make the initial call had to be well planned out and role played with someone who is experienced in reunions. It seemed like there would be a thousand scenarios that could have happened. Gina could have hung up on me. She could have chosen to keep the conversation to herself and not tell Becky about it. Or, she could have ignored the call and not ever called me back. I'm so thankful she did call me back. None of my story would have happened if she had not called me back. My faith was with me that day. One thing I am very sure of is that God was standing beside me the entire way.

My family has certainly grown over the past year. I keep going back to my forever dream of having a big family. That dream has come into reality. It's a good thing I keep a Day Planner. It's a great way to remember my new family's birthdays. Our journey is just beginning.

I am humbled that Ann's siblings often ask about me. They too are now a part of my big family even though we are not connected biologically. We are all connected at the heart.

Jackie, Becky and Gina are exceptional woman. We are all in our 60's. Basically, we were raised with the same values. When we were all together at our father's home, I remember my father kept thanking me for my perseverance in finding them. It was a very long journey but worth the wait. My father was proud to have his daughters together in his home. It is my dream to be able to spend more time with them to not only learn more about them but to make some memories to last the rest of our lives.

One thing I learned along the way about my adoption was how my biological paternal grandparents felt. My father had told me how upset they were that I was being relinquished. They felt that they were being stripped of having a relationship with me, their first born grandchild. I can certainly understand how they feel since I too am a grandparent. I would be devastated.

I also came to the realization of how much my adoptive father and biological father are somewhat alike. Both men are family men who would do anything for their families. These two men came from an era where men looked after their families first and foremost. They're both hard working men with amazing work ethics. Even though I have only met my biological father one time, I would do anything for him. Some children don't have any father figure in their lives. For me, I have been blessed having two fathers, two different but similar fathers who have loved me unconditionally.

It will take some time to learn more about my biological family. I can't wait to see what the future holds. I pray that my biological mother will want to meet me someday. This must be difficult for her. I hold no animosity towards her and my hope is to somehow help her heal. She gave me the greatest gift, the gift of a life every child deserves. I can't imagine how difficult it must have been for not only my biological mother to relinquish her daughter but for all the other mothers who have done the same thing.

Many questions I had concerning my medical family history have been answered. This is a very important topic for most adoptees. Meeting my biological family has answered many questions not only for myself but for my children and grandchildren. Why is Ben so tall? Now we know. Apparently it comes from his paternal grandfather. We've always wondered why Adam really didn't look like anyone in our family. Now we know. He favors his paternal grandfather. Why do I have arthritis in my hands? Now we know. It comes from my paternal side of my biological family. Other than just those few things, my biological parents are healthy, even in their 80's. That sure is a blessing!

My biological family is loving, compassionate and has tons of empathy. On several occasions Becky and Gina would say that they have put themselves in my shoes. They really took great strides in how I must have felt not only being adopted but finding my lost family after so many years. I too have put myself in their shoes to know what it feels like to have a full blood sister enter their lives out of the blue. One thing is for sure, we all understand. Our parents are human. That's something I can relate to as well. But on another note, my adoptive parents were too. Is it true we're a product of our environment? I think so. It shows not only for myself but for Ann as well. As I said at my mother's eulogy, "we are the lucky ones." With that being said, I think Ann and I turned out pretty well.

Acknowledgments

There are so many family members, friends and people I have met along my journey I have to thank for helping me in my journey.

GOD – To Him I give all the glory and thanks.

WILLIAM – His love and support is far more than I ever dreamed possible. He was by my side the entire way. He listened to me through my tears. His voice of reason kept my compass pointed in the right direction. Thank you for loving me, even when I ugly cry.

CAROL- She went above and beyond in helping me with my search. Carol has helped hundreds of adoptees reunite with her gifts and talents. She never gave up, even when several suspects fell through she persevered. Carol is truly an angel.

ANN- It's very rare that two adoptees find their biological family at the same time, especially at our age. I could not have done this without you. I'm thrilled to have held your hand while walking through the doors we went through on our journey. Know that your little sister loves you with all her heart.

ANCESTRY.COM- Thank you for developing the technology that provides those of us looking for answers about our families. I could have never found my family without your company. The enormous amount of records available were amazing to read and navigate.

23ANDME.COM- You were instrumental in giving me a complete understanding where my family originated from. Your technology traced my roots to places I never dreamed of and how they migrated through time. The medical information provided was truly amazing and put my mind to rest on hundreds of questions I had.

BEN and ADAM – God blessed me with you as my sons. Thank you for listening to me and for your support during this journey. Many questions we had have been answered. I'm certain we will have many more questions as time goes on. We will remain patient. God will reveal those answers. Thank you for my beautiful grandchildren. I love watching them bloom and grow.

CHERYL-You are my dearest friend. We've been friends for over 50 years. You have listened to me since high school when I first became inquisitive about my adoption and finding my biological family. I am eternally grateful. Thank you for your friendship, love and being a big part of my family.

JOHN- I wish others could see how much the light inside your heart shines like I do. My parents loved you like a son. Thank you for holding my mother's hand while she died. Thank you for staying at the hospital until William and I got there. Thank you being Ben and Adam's dad. You have shown them how to be men of honor.

PHIL, SUSAN AND MARANDA -Thank you for hosting me at your home to tell me your story. Your family is truly a great example of God's love and commitment to family.

JOYCE-You were the first biological cousin I met. Thank you for all the long talks we have had. You are a true inspiration and I'm glad you are a part of my life.

REBECCA LOUISE – Our relationship started at a bar when I blurted out that I was adopted. We became instant friends for the past few years. I was so blessed to have a front row seat while you first learned about your brother after years and years of searching for him. What a day of inspiration that was for me. It made me realize that I could never ever give up looking for my biological family. I'm so grateful to have you as my friend.

CHRISTINA RUOTOLO- Thank you for cheering me on to get this book started, finished, proof read and edited. Your talents never cease to amaze me. Your friendship through the last few years has meant more to me than words can say.

SHERRI HOLLISTER- Your wisdom has been a guiding force to getting this book published. I am eternally grateful.

PAMLICO WRITERS GROUP- This group of extremely talented local authors in Eastern North Carolina has inspired and educated me during the writing of Faith, Hope and Perseverance. Each and every one of you have truly been an inspiration to me. Thank you from the bottom of my heart.

PITT COUNTY WOMEN'S MAGAZINE- Aron and Amy Daniels, thank you for getting my first article published. This enabled my marketing campaign to get off to a whirl wind start. Keep doing great things and inspiring others.

DARIUS MOORE- Family Recruitment Specialist, Children's Home Society of North Carolina. We met at one of your informational seminars about foster to adoption. You were so very kind to allow me to be a participant during your presentation. I was truly impressed how you explained just what foster to adoption really was. The information you shared during about the Children's Home Society was truly amazing and concise. You were passionate about these children and their needs for a forever home. Keep up the great work and keep getting your message out. I'm glad we have gotten to know each other. Thank you for all you do.

CINDY KNUL – Statewide Recruitment Coordinator, Children's Home Society of North Carolina. You have so much room in your heart for children in foster care and adoption. Thank you for your friendship and inspiration.

MATT ANDERSON- Vice President, Programs and Business Development, Children's Home Society of North Carolina. Talking to you about CHS of NC gave me such a great understanding of the great work that you do. Thank you for your generosity and time and understanding.

JOYCE BAHR- President, Unsealed Initiative. On behalf of many, many adoptees, thank you for your hard work, your time and tenacity. It is because of you and your organization that adoptees born in New York state are now able to get an original certified copy of birth certificates. You are my hero!

ASSEMBLYMAN DAVID I. WEPRIN- Your decades of work towards getting the bill through for adoptees rights shows us your true dedication for our God given rights. Thank you for fighting for us.

SENATOR VELMANETTE MONTGOMERY- Thank you for being a major sponsor of the Clean Bill of Adoptee Rights. Thank you for your hard work and seeing this through to the end.

ANDREW M. CUOMO, GOVERNOR OF NEW YORK STATE-
God bless you for signing S3419/A5494 Adoptees Bill of Rights. You
certainly understand adoptees human rights. This 80 plus year old bill
is history that will return what is rightfully due adoptees of New York
State. I hope to meet you someday to personally thank you and tell you
exactly what this means not only me but to many adoptees.

TO MY NEW FOUND FAMILY- Thank you for accepting me.
Thank you for your love. I can't wait until we see each other again to
make beautiful memories.

**Here's to the thousands of close and distant family
I haven't met yet.
I hope to meet you soon!
ALL OF YOU HAVE MADE ME A BETTER PERSON.
I LOVE YOU ALL!**

About the Author

Diane Gray has always known she wanted to someday write a book but she could never figure out what to write about. So when she came back from New York in January, 2019, she decided that the story of finding her biological family was the one story she must write. It was such an emotional journey but her hope is to inspire others who are searching for their biological family.

Diane enjoyed an amazing career in advertising focusing on radio. When she was a few years away from retiring, she decided to pursue a dream of owning her own bridal boutique. She reached the magical retirement age, closed her bridal boutique and devoted much of her time to finding her biological family.

She is the proud mother of two sons, proud grandmother of three children and "bonus mom" to a daughter and son and a fur baby named Owen. Diane and her husband live in Eastern North Carolina and you can find them relaxing and having fun at their home "down at the crik".

Diane is also available to be a guest speaker for any organization that may need a presenter. You can contact her at fhpspeaker@yahoo.com.

CPSIA information can be obtained
at www.ICGtesting.com
Printed in the USA
LVHW050932050720
659739LV00004B/281